Jesus' Table Talk

Jesus' Table Talk

Insights into How to Engage Our Culture Today

Scott Townsend

Foreword by Noel Sanderson

WIPF & STOCK · Eugene, Oregon

JESUS' TABLE TALK
Insights into How to Engage Our Culture Today

Copyright © 2019 Scott Townsend. All rights reserved. Except for brief quotations in critical publications or reviews, no part of this book may be reproduced in any manner without prior written permission from the publisher. Write: Permissions, Wipf and Stock Publishers, 199 W. 8th Ave., Suite 3, Eugene, OR 97401.

Wipf & Stock
An Imprint of Wipf and Stock Publishers
199 W. 8th Ave., Suite 3
Eugene, OR 97401

www.wipfandstock.com

PAPERBACK ISBN: 978-1-5326-7340-5
HARDCOVER ISBN: 978-1-5326-7341-2
EBOOK ISBN: 978-1-5326-7342-9

Manufactured in the U.S.A.   APRIL 1, 2019

This book is dedicated to my wife and children. Thank you for all the wonderful table conversations we've had through the years.

Contents

Foreword by Noel Sanderson | ix
Acknowledgements | xi

        Introduction | 1
One   Banquets and Symposia in First-Century Israel | 11
Two   Eating with Tax Collectors and Sinners: A Banquet | 18
Three The Party Crasher: A Symposium | 35
Four   The One with the Woes: A Symposium | 51
Five   The Seat of Humility: A Symposium | 65
Six   The Last Supper: A Symposium? | 78
Seven A Meal with Two Disciples | 92
Eight From Jesus' Table to Ours | 101
Nine Conclusion | 117

Bibliography | 121

Foreword

THE BIRTH OF JESUS Christ, the Son of God, Messiah, did not happen in a cultural, political, or religious vacuum. Jesus of Nazareth was born into a Jewish family, immersed and schooled in first-century Judaism, and in a region under the control of the Roman Empire, ruled by cruel and corrupt client-kings. It was a dangerous time and life was uncertain, the social order of the day riven with multiple layers of division. In the midst of those times, Jesus grew up in a family and would have experienced a very typical upbringing for a Jewish boy with a carpenter for a father. His childhood would, in my view, have been an important foundation for the later years when he engaged so courageously and compassionately with the complex multitude of humanity living all around in Samaria, Judea, and Galilee.

The fact that the heavenly Father chose a family, Joseph and Mary, to not only birth the Messiah but take responsibility for parenting Jesus through all the stages of nurture, including religious education, should not be lost on any Christian. Before Jesus was a rabbi, he was an infant, a toddler, a child, and part of a family. He would have had many meals at a table; after all, Joseph was a carpenter. How much of Jesus' religious and social worldview was shaped by unrecorded conversations, we may never know. Nevertheless, Scott Townsend has reminded us of the critical role of family interactions in shaping our foundational understanding of our own complex context.

Foreword

Scott Townsend has re-introduced his readers to the significance of conversations Jesus had at the meal tables of the first century. He has highlighted the interplay between the many voices that would have been heard at those tables: the Greeks, the Romans, the religious and irreligious, the outcasts and self-described insiders, the broken and self-made, the rich, the poor, the sinners, and the genuine seekers of eternal life. Along the way, he has offered his readers opportunities to consider the meaning and significance of these conversations for their own times and contexts. Whether the reader agrees with Townsend's personal understanding of those conversations or not, he has drawn our attention to the underlying missional intentionality of Jesus, to break with righteous hypocrisy in pursuit of the inestimably valuable human soul.

To understanding Jesus' social interactions, the times and culture of his day must be better grasped than is commonly the case in contemporary Christianity, certainly in the West. Here, Scott Townsend has opened a window in the often subtle or less explained cultural nuances of the time. From what it meant to offer hospitality in your home, to the silent signals sent to both the guest and the observers, Townsend offers readers important clues to interpreting not just what was said in a conversation, but what was meant in the exchanges, including the symbolic placing of guests around the table. Stepping back from the immediate context of each table, one has the opportunity of distilling the conversation to the essence of how Jesus used each scene to advance the mission of God with love, courage, and compassion.

One may be tempted to ask whether we may learn anything of real value from the meals Jesus had with all the diverse people discussed in this book. The short answer must surely be a resounding yes. Nothing Jesus said or did can simply be relegated to a dusty shelf in the ancient history section of a library. Despite the historical context in which Jesus lived his earthly life, the timeless truths teased out of each encounter by Scott Townsend points us to the everlasting love of God for all human beings.

Noel Sanderson

Acknowledgements

THIS BOOK WAS BORN from a conversation I had with a visiting professor at Trinity Bible College and Graduate School. The professor spoke on biblical leadership, but after some conversations, he indicated an interesting study of symposia in the Gospel of Luke. From that time on for the next two years, I have been writing this book, growing more in my interest in Jewish culture both as represented in the Bible as well as represented throughout history. Along with this, my interest in family and youth ministry helped to fuel this study. Particularly studies that helped to inform the importance of family engagement, and particularly around the dinner table. My interest in Jewish culture, the family, and the dinner table helped to birth this book.

Throughout the study of the passages in this book, I learned important lessons that I try to exemplify in my own family and ministry life. My prayer is that as you read this book you too will be inspired and challenged to make Jesus' table talk an important part of your family and community dining experience.

Introduction

DINNERS AROUND THE FAMILY table are an important part of family life and health, not just for physical sustenance; when practiced regularly, family dinners help to provide valuable benefits, spiritually and relationally, for those involved.[1] For instance, the survey results from the Center on Addiction survey, conducted in 2012, indicated that frequent dinners practiced together by family members helped the young people in the family to make better, safer decisions, and were less likely to engage in destructive behavior.[2] I'm all for helping my children not engage in destructive behavior, and if spending quality time together as a family helps to curtail that, let's eat! Interestingly, the dinner table has played an important role in many cultures including the development of morality and social orderliness.[3] As members of the family and members of the cultural community eat together, there is a fortification and even a modification of social orderliness.[4]

For many people today in a Western context, the practice of eating together is becoming a scarcity due to conflicting schedules and interests.[5] However, in a Western context, with the diversity of cultures represented, the table is utilized in a variety of ways.[6]

1. "Importance of Family Dinners VII," 6
2. "Importance of Family Dinners VII," 6.
3. Ochs and Shohet, "Cultural Structuring of Mealtime Socialization," 35–49.
4. Ochs and Shohet, "Cultural Structuring of Mealtime Socialization," 36.
5. Ochs and Shohet, "Cultural Structuring of Mealtime Socialization," 38.
6. Ochs and Shohet, "Cultural Structuring of Mealtime Socialization," 38.

Jesus' Table Talk

For instance, some cultures eat together as family, while others separate into groups to eat.[7] I am a member of the X Generation. We were the first latchkey kids whose parents both worked, if we had both parents in the house, while we were raised in daycare or in front of the television.[8] Our family dinners often consisted of frozen dinners on a tray in front of our favorite TV program. Sometimes I felt like I knew more about the family members in *Silver Spoons* than I did about my own family.

Regardless, those who partake in the experience of eating together away from the physical dinner table consider the value of the experience to be similar to that of eating around the dinner table. Meaning, if our family eats together in the living room rather than the dining room, the impact is the same.[9] Growing up as a Generation Xer, television was the center of the home. As a family (a broken family: my mother and father divorced when I was very young), my mother, sister, and I would eat together while watching our favorite TV shows. However, my mother was also attending university, so often my sister and I were left to fend for ourselves while she worked or studied. Does that count?

What This Book is About

This book will guide the reader through a variety of passages of Scripture recorded in the Gospel of Luke that placed Jesus at the dinner table. The stories represented in the passages of Scripture demonstrate a number of situations either into which Jesus was thrust, or into which he placed himself. After all, he was, and is, the Son of God. Was he ever really "thrust" into a situation? Likely not. When I find myself "thrust" into situations, I can often become a bit discombobulated, depending on the context. That's not quite how we see Jesus represented in the Gospels.

---

7. Ochs and Shohet, "Cultural Structuring of Mealtime Socialization," 38.
8. Andert, "Alternating Leadership," 72.
9. Parker-Pope, "Family Meal is What Counts."

INTRODUCTION

Some of the situations, such as Jesus dining with Levi, the tax collector, and Levi's friends, placed Jesus in a seemingly questionable situation that garnered Jesus references of being a "glutton and a drunkard."[10] For some believers in our contemporary church culture, the notion that Jesus would have attended any gathering where there could have been alcohol seems implausible at best and downright heretical if not even demonic at worst, despite what we read, though, that Jesus created wine at the wedding at Cana.[11] Some contemporary followers of Jesus attempt to excuse this creation of wine as some kind of perfect-tasting grape juice. In spite of the fact, however, that the host of the wedding party indicated that this was the best wine, the kind that would be brought out first among the guests to get them drunk, and then bring out the cheap wine at the end of the wedding party when they would be too inebriated to care about taste.[12]

At another dinner to which Jesus was invited, the first symposium mentioned by Luke, a woman crashed the dinner party and behaved rather crudely by kissing Jesus' feet, crying her tears on and wiping his feet with her hair that was likely hanging loosely.[13] Was this a scandalous demonstration on the woman's part, or could there be other reasons why she did what she did? Simon the Pharisee's response that if Jesus only knew who she was he would not let her continue doing what she was doing, was not unlike many of our responses might be had a similar scene occurred in our homes today.[14]

Reading passages in their historical context as those introduced above, you may consider the conclusion that Jesus was willing to place himself in situations that appeared controversial—even looked forward to it. Although that may not be far from the truth, many believers today find that to be not only unlikely but also difficult to believe. As Leonard Sweet has said in his book,

10. Luke 7:34 (NIV).
11. John 2:1–12.
12. John 2:10.
13. Luke 7:36–50.
14. Luke 7:39.

The Bad Habits of Jesus, "Would Jesus offend you today? If not you are missing the scandalous nature of Jesus, the rebel rousing rabbi as told in the stories of the Gospels."[15] Rebel rouser? Could my Jesus be a rebel rouser? Well, yes, at least according to some of the religious leaders, and others, of Jesus' day.

I recall when I was in college and interning at a church in our state. During the summers, the church district with which I am affiliated held a family camp for families to come and enjoy some camp ministry for the whole family. During one family camp the speaker asked the question, "Was Jesus ever spanked?" Of course, our thoughts often move straight to, "Absolutely not! He was the Son of God, the Perfect Man!" However, the speaker discussed the options he suggested, that is, could Jesus have done something that his parents found to be disobedient? After all, in the Gospels, there are several people, Pharisees and scribes, who considered Jesus to be disobedient. So, could Jesus have ever been spanked by his parents? Sure. The point is, sometimes we as Christians have an image of Jesus that was not held by the people of his day, including his parents, his disciples, not to mention the Pharisees and scribes. He looked, dressed, and smelled just like everyone else.

You may recall the scene recorded in Mark 3:21, 31–35. Jesus' mother and brothers arrived to collect him. Verse 21 records that his family went to gather Jesus because, "He is out of his mind."[16] Jesus' own family thought he was going crazy. In an honor and shame culture like that of first-century Israel, the family's fear would likely have been that Jesus was bringing shame upon the house. Moxnes's comments on honor and shame in his article, "Honor and Shame" when he says:

> [H]onor conferred on the basis of virtuous deeds is called *acquired* honor. By its very nature acquired honor may be either gained or lost in the perpetual struggle for public recognition. Since the group is so important for the identity of a Mediterranean . . . it is critical to

---

15. Sweet, *Bad Habits of Jesus*, xv.
16. Mark 3:21 (NIV).

recognize that honor status comes primarily from *group* recognition.[17]

Jesus was, according to his family, behaving in a shameful way and they came to gather him up and take him back home where he belonged. He was obviously suffering from a Messiah complex.

Jesus was, for all intents and purposes, human. However, what his family in particular, and the Jews in general didn't realize was that the intent and purpose of Jesus' life on earth was to finish the job that God called the Jews to, to be a light to the world and ultimately to redeem not only Israel, but all of humanity and creation.[18] Unfortunately, though, we as a church often find ourselves disconnected from the intent and purpose of Jesus.

The Contemporary Church

One of the issues that the contemporary church faces is that its members are often considered too sheltered from those outside the church that really need Jesus.[19] Often, some believers in the church prefer to be safe and sound inside our church building, away from the influence of those people outside. It seems that those believers do not really understand what is going on in the world of the unbeliever, some people outside the church may say. Christians are only concerned about getting an unbeliever saved, nothing more. The less time they have to hang around dirty unbelievers the better.[20] I have encountered believers who seem to believe that it is better to stay away from *the world* and the *effects of the world* for fear of being sucked in to the dangers of the *dark side*. I understand the fear, and I'm not trying to make too light of it. But we seem to forget that "You . . . are from God and have overcome them, because the one who is in you is greater than who is in the world."[21]

---

17. Moxnes, "Honor and Shame," 20.
18. Wright, *Surprised by Hope*, 197.
19. Kinnaman and Lyons, *UnChristian*, 122.
20. Kinnaman and Lyons, *UnChristian*, 67–69.
21. 1 John 4:4, NIV.

In some cases, it seems that some believers' lack of interaction with the world is motivated by fear. I can recall my experiences as an undergraduate at my alma mater in the class "Personal Evangelism." A requirement of the class was to knock on people's doors that we did not know, introduce them to Jesus through what was called the *two question test* and, hopefully, lead them to Jesus. This was not an easy exercise, and, frankly, fear often prompted me to cut the questions short, much to the satisfaction of the unfortunate person I was questioning on their doorstep.

In our day, door-to-door evangelism, or *man on the street* evangelism, where people are surveyed to lead them to recognize their need for Jesus, simply does not work the way they may have in the distant past. Most people today, in our Western context, do not come to know Jesus because of evangelistic efforts, but because of good conversations and relationships.[22] If this is the case, what is stopping us from sharing a proverbial meal with people who don't know Jesus, building relationships with them, and demonstrating to them the life and words of Jesus? If it is fear, we must keep in mind the exhortation Paul gave to Timothy in 2 Timothy 1:7 (NIV), "For the Spirit God gave us does not make us timid, but gives us power, love and self-discipline."

I often found myself reading the 2 Timothy passage and wondering why God hadn't changed my fear factor. I still found myself nervous to talk to people about Jesus, to meet people and strike up a conversation about what Jesus has done in my life and theirs. However, what I believe Paul didn't mean in the 2 Timothy passage was that once we become followers of Jesus we are suddenly fearless, endowed with power, love, and self-control. If that were the case we would have a lot less need for Christian counselors. I believe what Paul meant was that God does not give us a Spirit that makes us fearful. The fear we experience is of our own making. We have access to his Spirit that provides us with power, love, and self-control. Ultimately, I believe what this means is that we need to be disciplined to reach out to our neighbors about the love of Jesus in spite of fear and doubt.

---

22. McLaren, *More Ready than You Realize*, 14.

INTRODUCTION

What these table passages in Luke illustrate is that Jesus seemed to be comfortable spending time with sinners, prostitutes, and even tax collectors. Not only was he comfortable, he seemed to welcome the opportunity to sit with those who the religiously segregated considered to be outsiders. What has changed since Jesus' time that the church is unwilling to engage with people in need?

Only fairly recently the church has become synonymous with disengagement with the culture.[23] The more Christians attempt to engage with culture, the more they are seen, mostly by those in the church, as compromisers, flirting with the devil. It seems, sometimes, that when people in the church talk about ministry or evangelism, they really want to keep it in the church. I can't count the number of times churches I attended brought in evangelists to preach to the church, not to the prostitutes, the sinners, or even the tax collectors. When we start doing ministry *outside* we run the risk of bringing some of the world's problems into our house, and that just can't be.

A friend of mine who worked as a youth pastor wanted to bring young people into the church who were not acquainted with the church or church behavior. His desire was to reach those who have not yet been reached. The parents of the church didn't like the influence of "bad kids" tainting their kids' experience in the church. In the end, he was fired.

A caveat here is to recognize that Jesus did not view his position as standing between the dry and stuffy religious in contrast to the needs of the world. His position was not to set right the fundamentalists, also known as Pharisees, and become the voice of the marginalized, the poor, the sick, and the disenfranchised. Rather, Jesus' position was that of the Messiah, the one who came to faithfully administer the promise given to Abraham and his descendants, the Israelites, as a blessing to the whole world.[24] As such it is less of a division between the world and the believers and rather a setting right of the world by shining the light of Jesus into all parts of the world.

23. Kinnaman and Lyons, *UnChristian*, 124.
24. Wright, *Surprised by Hope*, 197.

Are You an Epicurean Gnostic?

What seems to have happened is a dichotomy between spirituality and what is referred to as The World connoting sinful humanity and things to stay away from. The denomination to which I belong used to have rules and regulations preventing their members from attending movie theaters, swimming in public pools with the opposite sex, and prescribed hair and clothing styles for men and women. Although some of these regulations are not all bad, in and of themselves, the purpose for them was to establish a sense of purity among themselves and from the world.

This view seems to have more in common with Epicureanism and Gnosticism than with Christianity. Epicureanism regards a division between the physical and the non-physical. Epicureanism regards God or the gods as entirely uninvolved in creation.[25] If there is a God, or gods, He, She, or they are disassociated with the world and uninterested in it.[26] Gnosticism, which in some ways has more to do with Christianity today than does Scripture, it seems, regards the physical to be of less importance, even evil, whereas the spiritual is good, preferred.[27] A modern Christian Epicurean Gnostic may say something like the following: "It is either God or the World, we can't have both!" That is, the Epicurean perspective is that God is not involved in the world, and a Gnostic perspective is that the world is sinful, so why would God be involved in the world, and so why should we as Christians be involved in the world? These Greek worldviews have become central in the worldview of the modern Western culture including Western Christians. God and the spiritual are good; the world and the physical are bad and in the end will be ultimately destroyed as we who are believers will continue on with God, spiritually, forever.

The Jewish perspective of creation and the world was less dualistic and more holistic. In other words, God, as the Creator, created a world that was good (Gen 1:31). After creation, sin entered

---

25. Wright, *Surprised by Scripture*, 8.
26. Wright, *Surprised by Scripture*, 8.
27. King, *What is Gnosticism?*, 8.

INTRODUCTION

the world through his creation, the first man and woman, whom Genesis refers to as *the man* and *the woman* (Gen 2-3). With sin a part of not only humanity but all of creation, God's plan was not to simply redeem humanity, but all of creation as well.[28] Paul, in Romans 8:22-23 (NIV), stated this when he wrote, "We know that the whole creation has been groaning as in the pains of childbirth right up to the present time. Not only so, but we ourselves, who have the firstfruits of the Spirit, groan inwardly as we wait eagerly for our adoption to sonship, the redemption of our bodies." Jesus' death and resurrection became the first fruit not only for the redemption of humanity but for the renewal of all of creation.

Francis Schaeffer, in his seminal work, *The God Who is There*, suggested that Christian theology and practice has moved from verifiable truth to existential, non-verifiable, leaps of faith.[29] Moving in this direction, the church is no longer able, logically and rationally, to engage with culture in a way that is meaningful.[30] As the church has continued to live in such a way as to be disengaged with culture, a sense of judgment against that which does not conform to the church's perception of what is true and right has developed leaving a disengaged, judgmental, sheltered church.[31] The notion of a contemporary believer spending time with someone outside of the church, particularly someone with a questionable reputation, is unthinkable.

As I am writing this, a student in our graduate school sent me a link to an article in the *Huffington Post*. The article, entitled "My Evangelical Church is Gaslighting Me, But I Refuse to Fall for it Anymore,"[32] addressed the issue this Christian woman faced as her political perspective began to shift away from a Republican orientation to a more moderate, or dare I say, Democratic orientation. The author of this article admitted to at one time having a strong faith in Jesus and even the church. However, with the current

---

28. Hahne, *Corruption and Redemption of Creation*, 2.
29. Schaeffer, *Trilogy*, 51-55.
30. Schaeffer, *Trilogy*, 53.
31. Kinnaman and Lyons, *UnChristian*, 183.
32. Baker, "My Evangelical Church is Gaslighting Me."

political climate in America, she saw the Christians she thought she knew support a presidential candidate, and now a president who did not seem to live up to the faith in Jesus he espoused. At least he's a Republican and getting the job done for us as Christians. If we, along with this woman, step away from the issue presented to us as believers and attempt to look at it a bit objectively, we may see that we are reflecting the Pharisees and the scribes of the first century, trying to get the right person on the throne to kick out the evildoers so we can once again be the political and religious force in the world. That didn't work well for them and it won't work well for us today either.

My desire is to encourage the reader to come back to what is important, the table, but more importantly, to recognize the importance of engaging people around a proverbial table with whom you may not normally associate. The purpose of this book is to challenge your thinking as a believer regarding people's needs and how you might meet them, and to challenge your view of contemporary Christianity and the hypocrisy with which we are so often accused. Finally, I hope to make Jesus' table talk a welcome part of your faith and life as a believer.

One

Banquets and Symposia in First-Century Israel

IF YOU COULD STEP into an average American home during dinnertime, it is likely you will see something similar to the following scenario. Mom or dad has made dinner (or bought dinner at one of the local fast-food restaurants available), consisting of something quick and easy because, after all, everyone is busy and in a hurry with more important things to do. The family wanders into the kitchen to grab their food and sits down around the TV. As the children finish their food they take their plate to the kitchen, if they feel so inclined, and head to their rooms to do homework, call friends, watch their own TV, or browse the world through their smartphones and tablets. Although this may, in part, reflect the average American household, it is not necessarily the ideal way to enjoy family fellowship.

Contrast the eating habits of TV families through the years. Consider *Leave it to Beaver* with their happy homemaker wife who had dinner ready and on the table when her husband came home from a hard day's work. Today's TV shows would be hard-pressed to want to have a dinner setting as mundane, antiquated, and suburban as *Leave it to Beaver*. Is it art imitating reality, or reality imitating art?

Eating practices in first-century Israel looked considerably different than they do today, particularly in Western cultures. The center of the home, it seems, for many in the West is the television.[1] As such, families tend to gravitate not around the dinner table, but around the TV set. One study indicated that children watch on average two-and-a-half to three hours of TV per day, with the content of the programming being questionable for some kids viewing.[2] This does not account for the amount of time children engage with electronic screens other than the television, such as tablets, smartphones, and the like, rather than connecting with relationships in their own home.[3] Leonard Sweet, in his book, *From Tablet to Table: Where Community is Found and Identity is Formed*, expressed concern about the TV's place among the American family. He stated:

> When we divorce ourselves from the table, we lose a lot in the settlement; the food we settle for is not only less nutritious and more potentially harmful, it is also fundamentally less satisfying . . . No wonder we redirect our attention from the food to the television.[4]

It may come as no surprise that families who own more than one TV seem to spend less time together, compromising family bonds.[5] That said, if the center of the family home in Western cultures is the TV, less time is spent talking and sharing with one another.[6] In contrast to this, however, a study reported by the *New York Times* in 2007 indicated that whether families ate together in front of the TV or at the dinner table was essentially irrelevant; it was the act of eating together that was important.[7] However, I have to ask myself how many families that were studied spent time talking with one another in spite of the TV, or even because of the TV?

---

1. Sweet, *From Tablet to Table*, 10.
2. Dorey et al., "Children and Television Watching," 414–20.
3. Dorey et al., "Children and Television Watching," 415.
4. Sweet, *From Tablet to Table*, 79.
5. Dorey et al., "Children and Television Watching," 419.
6. "Importance of Family Dinners VII," 1.
7. Parker-Pope, "Family Meal is What Counts."

Regardless of your opinion on the benefits or dangers of television, the table in the family home is important. Sweet, again, argues for the benefits of the dining table when he says, "The table is where we learn protocols of the table, and houseways of the home, which become protocols of life."[8] Elinor Ochs and Merav Shohet, in their article, "The Cultural Structuring of Mealtime Socialization," said, in agreement with Sweet:

> Mealtimes are both vehicles for and end points of culture. As vehicles, mealtimes constitute universal occasions for members not only to engage in the activities of feeding and eating but also to forge relationships that reinforce or modify the social order.[9]

How many times have you sat at the table with your family and through some conversations, or sibling disagreement, discussed an important life lesson that extended beyond the table?

Contrast our hyper-entertainment culture with that of first-century Israel. The center of the home for the first-century Palestinian was not the television, but the table.[10] Think about it, there was no TV, no Xbox, and no movie theaters. What was there? The table.

Early First-Century Table Practices

The table in the first century for Jews in Roman-occupied Israel was influenced by what is referred to as the Roman triclinium.[11] The word *triclinium* comes from the Greek description of three couches.[12] Jesus and his contemporaries observed the eating practices of the triclinium as it is referred to in several passages (i.e. Luke 13:29; John 13:23). The triclinium was a series of couches

---

8. Sweet, *From Tablet to Table*, 101.

9. Ochs and Shohet, "Cultural Structuring of Mealtime Socialization," 35–36.

10. Ochs and Shohet, "Cultural Structuring of Mealtime Socialization," 37.

11. Klein, "Torah in *Triclinia*," 332.

12. Klein, "Torah in *Triclinia*," 332.

typically set in an upside down 'U' shape with a small table in front of them.[13] The couches were set on the floor, sometimes with soft cushions, and the tables were short tables off which the guests would eat. The guests would recline at the table on their left arm while eating and drinking with their right arm.[14] Typically, there were three guests set at each side of the couch so nine people would be sat around the table. The order of the attendants and the couches was important as well. As a spectator, looking at the table with the two ends immediately facing you, the couch on the left was the highest couch, the couch on the top middle was the medium couch, and the couch on the right was the lowest couch.[15]

The setup of the couches and their positions was not designated by actual height, but rather by social importance.[16] Since there were three couches, the guest of honor would have been placed at the high couch, to the left of the host, adjacent to the medium couch, while the host would have been placed in the middle of the guest of honor and an honored guest who would be sat at the right of the host.[17] The setup of the couches, and where guests sat, indicated their importance socially.[18] If a guest sat in a particular spot around the triclinium, that guest would know immediately where his importance lay with the group gathered for the banquet. This is similar to seating at junior and high school cafeterias. Certain groups in the cafeteria are the cool kids who sit at a particular table, certain groups are the nerds at another table, and certain groups are the geeks, and so on. As in the school cafeteria, so also around the first-century table in Israel, it is unwise to try to cross the social boundaries in a setting like this for fear of retribution.

Along with invited guests, at times uninvited guests would appear at the table, or at least at the host's home.[19] In the first

13. Klein, "Torah in *Triclinia*," 332.
14. Klein, "Torah in *Triclinia*," 332.
15. Klein, "Torah in *Triclinia*," 332.
16. Klein, "Torah in *Triclinia*," 332.
17. Klein, "Torah in *Triclinia*," 332.
18. Thacker, "Three Concepts of Tolerance," 67–68.
19. Marshall, "Jesus," 50.

century, particularly in the homes of affluent members of society, an open dwelling plan was designed to allow uninvited guests to wander in off the streets.[20] The uninvited guests could walk into the house, even the living area, and watch the banquet take place as a spectator of sorts.[21]

Take some time to reflect on this. You are sitting at the table with your family or entertaining some important guests and in wanders some onlookers watching the dinner party. They are not invited but they are allowed to simply watch as the dinner festivities unfold. For me the word *uncomfortable* comes to mind.

Banquets and Symposia

For the sake of this book, there will be two primary dinner practices discussed. They are the banquet and the symposium. Banquets like those recorded in Luke 5:27–39 and Luke 22:14–38 were celebratory gatherings. Symposia like those recorded in Luke 7:36–50, Luke 11:37–54, and Luke 14:1–24 were intended to be teaching banquets, particularly for the wealthy and religious leadership of Jesus' day.

The symposia recorded in Luke were geared toward teaching, learning, and discovery. The Greek and Roman cultures, from where the Jews borrowed the symposia, tended to look significantly different than a Jewish symposium. A symposium, for members of a Greek or Roman culture, may have been a time of festivity, or in other cases, little less than an orgy with food.[22] Remember the *dinner party* at which Herod's daughter was dancing and during which Herod's wife and daughter asked for the head of John the Baptist (Matt 14:6–12)? This would have been a symposium for the Romans, as Herod took a perverted pleasure watching his daughter dance. What I find particularly interesting is that the Jews didn't distance themselves from the symposium; rather they

---

20. Marshall, "Jesus," 50.
21. Marshall, "Jesus," 51.
22. Smith, *From Symposium to Eucharist*, 12.

embraced it, using it for the best it could be, a time of teaching and learning. How often have you heard churches or believers preach the importance of distancing ourselves from the world for fear of appearing compromising. Here, the Jews, rather than distancing themselves from Roman and Greek culture, embraced what was part of a pagan, gentile culture, and celebrated the benefits of the practice of the symposium.

Today we use the word *symposium* to designate a conference or teaching session. In some ways, this is what the first-century Jewish symposium was. The banquets were simply that, banquets. These were times of celebration or gathering. The symposia, however, were special gatherings, typically of social and religious elite, with the chief guest invited because of his wisdom.[23] These gatherings were held at the table, in a banquet-style, with the intention of discussing important religious and social issues of the day.

This should not come as a surprise to us. One of the prayers the Jews would pray both morning and night was the Shema.[24] The Shema, taken from Deuteronomy and Leviticus, was a reminder for the faithful Jew to teach and learn God's word in every part of their day with one another, learning about and worshiping God through the study of his word, his Torah. In what ways could this dedication to God and the study of his word benefit us as gentile Christians in our relationship with one another and with God?

In the next chapter, the banquet of a known tax collector will be highlighted. Jesus invited this tax collector, Levi, to follow him and be his disciple. In turn, Levi invited Jesus to a banquet—a party.

Questions for Reflection:

1. Think about the time you and your family eat together. Do you eat around the dinner table? Around the television? Why?

---

23. Klein, "Torah in Triclinia," 339.
24. Tverberg, *Walking in the Dust of Rabbi Jesus*, 31.

2. If you eat around the dinner table, do you take time to provide learning opportunities for your family? How?

3. If you eat around the television, do you take time to discuss the elements of the show you are watching? Consider talking about how you as a Christian family can engage with people like those you are watching on TV.

Two

Eating with Tax Collectors and Sinners

A Banquet

LUKE 5:27–39 (NIV)

After this, Jesus went out and saw a tax collector by the name of Levi sitting at his tax booth. "Follow me," Jesus said to him, and Levi got up, left everything and followed him. Then Levi held a great banquet for Jesus at his house, and a large crowd of tax collectors and others were eating with them. But the Pharisees and the teachers of the law who belonged to their sect complained to his disciples, "Why do you eat and drink with tax collectors and sinners?" Jesus answered them, "It is not the healthy who need a doctor, but the sick. I have not come to call the righteous, but sinners to repentance." They said to him, "John's disciples often fast and pray, and so do the disciples of the Pharisees, but yours go on eating and drinking." Jesus answered, "Can you make the friends of the bridegroom fast while he is with them? But the time will come when the bridegroom will be taken from them; in those days they will fast." He told them this parable: "No one tears a piece out of a new garment to patch an old one. Otherwise, they will have torn the new garment, and the patch from the new will not match the old. And no one pours new wine into old wineskins. Otherwise, the new wine will burst the skins; the wine will run out and the wineskins will be ruined. No, new wine must be

Eating with Tax Collectors and Sinners

poured into new wineskins. And no one after drinking old wine wants the new, for they say, 'The old is better.'"

An anecdote told by one of my coworkers indicated that at a recent meeting of Pentecostals from a particular denomination, the question of whether Christians should be allowed to drink alcohol made its way to the agenda. After much heated discussion, the conclusion of the matter went something like this: "My Lord would never be caught drinking alcohol, let alone make alcohol for others to drink!" Whether this story is true or not, likely you have heard someone say something like this, or you yourself have said it. Often that response is given to passages like the one above, and more particularly about Jesus turning water into wine at the wedding in Cana (John 2). Never mind that the issue at hand is not about alcohol. As is often the case, we as modern Western Christians focus on a minor element of the story and make it one of importance, if not the most important issue of the story. So what is the main point?

Many people in our churches, particularly Pentecostal churches that tend toward an American holiness perspective, would have a difficult time accepting that Jesus was hanging out with people that first-century Jewish culture considered to be questionable at best and utterly sinful at worst.

Who Were the Tax Collectors?

In this passage, we read that Jesus, seen as a rabbi by many, called Levi, a tax collector, to follow him. Would that have been so bad? Who were the tax collectors? What did it mean to be called to be a disciple in the first century? Tax collectors during Jesus' day were normally Jews who would collect taxes of various kinds.[1] Often tax collectors needed to be from the Jewish population because they were more aware of Jewish customs and culture than their Roman counterparts were.[2] In other words, the Romans trusted

---

1. Young, *Jesus the Jewish Theologian*, 181–89.
2. Young, *Jesus the Jewish Theologian*, 181–89.

the Jewish tax collectors to know how to rip off and take advantage of their fellow Jews and the Jewish tax collectors were all too happy to oblige. Since the Jewish tax collectors associated with unclean Roman gentiles, they also were considered unclean and were despised by other Jews.[3] They were also despised because tax collectors, even Jewish ones, were prone to extortion and tax hikes for the sake of personal financial gain.[4] Stories were told of tax collectors carrying off relatives of the deceased who owed taxes, beating the relative until they paid the dues of their deceased loved ones.[5] Needless to say, tax collectors had a questionable reputation at best. In the Luke passage, Jesus called a tax collector to be his disciple. Can you imagine the emotions of those watching Jesus, and finding out that he called a tax collector to be a disciple? What about Levi's response? He simply got up and followed Jesus. Levi was likely aware enough of Jewish custom to understand the significance of being called to be a disciple by a rabbi.

Jewish tax collectors in the Gospels were continuously associated with sinners. Sinners in the Gospels were not simply references to sinful people, but people whom knowingly and willingly sinned. Frequently, in the Gospels, tax collectors and sinners were mentioned together.

> Matthew 11:19 (NIV): The Son of Man came eating and drinking, and they say, 'Here is a glutton and a drunkard, a friend of tax collectors and sinners.' But wisdom is proved right by her deeds.

> Mark 2:16 (NIV): When the teachers of the law who were Pharisees saw him eating with the sinners and tax collectors, they asked his disciples: 'Why does he eat with tax collectors and sinners?'

> Luke 15:1 (NIV): Now the tax collectors and sinners were all gathering around to hear Jesus.

---

3. Young, *Jesus the Jewish Theologian*, 181–89.
4. Young, *Jesus the Jewish Theologian*, 181–89.
5. Cavanaugh, "Private Tax Collectors."

Eating with Tax Collectors and Sinners

The implication is that tax collectors were not regarded any higher than sinners were by Jews, let alone by the Pharisees.

In 2008, Bernard Madoff was arrested for orchestrating one of the largest Ponzi schemes in American history.[6] Madoff said he was investing money for clients, but while taking their money, he garnered money from new clients to make false payouts to other clients. This scheme made him a billionaire, but also cost him life in prison. Can you imagine someone like the late Billy Graham asking Madoff to come alongside him as a follower, a disciple? What kind of questions would you have for Billy Graham? What kind of doubts would you have about what he taught? Would you be able to take what Billy Graham said seriously after finding out he brought on as a disciple someone as questionable as Bernard Madoff?

Although Levi may not have been involved in Ponzi schemes per se, he nonetheless took money from fellow Jews and probably a lot of it. By likely charging exorbitant amounts on taxes, as was common for tax collectors, his fellow Jews were often not able to give their tithe to the temple.[7] By virtue of his occupation, he was still viewed as despicable, untrustworthy, and despised. In spite of Levi's occupation and reputation, Jesus called him to be his disciple. What does that mean to you? Jesus—who had been demonstrating a significant level of understanding of the Torah and communicating the Torah in such a way as to amaze his listeners (nobody taught like Jesus)—did something like this, and called a Jew who made himself like a gentile, Levi, the tax collector. However, Jesus looked beyond the stigma of culture that Levi lived with and saw something useful as one of his followers. Do you find yourself at times feeling like an outsider? Someone who does not seem to fit in?

Remember the story of David, as a young shepherd boy. Samuel, in 1 Samuel 16, traveled to Bethlehem and asked Jesse, David's father, to bring out his sons. Jesse did so, but neglected to bring David to the lineup; after all, he was just a shepherd and

---

6. Ahamed, "How Bernard Madoff Did It."
7. Levine, *Short Stories by Jesus*, 189.

the youngest of his sons. God told Samuel not to consider their appearance since he had rejected them. Despite looking kingly and impressive, God did not choose them as Saul's successor. Reluctantly Jesse brought out David, the shepherd. He was young, unimpressive, and, well, a shepherd. However, God, despite appearances, looked at David's heart and chose David.

I find myself imagining a scene from a movie (after all, I am a Generation Xer raised in front of the television) with several strapping, burly brothers standing in a row, trying to look manlier than the next. In walks David, a little dirty from being out in the field, maybe with a lamb following behind him, asking his father why he was called to the meeting. Then, the respected sage, Samuel, points at David and says, "It's you, you're going to be the next king of Israel." At which time Samuel anoints David's head while his brothers, red-faced with anger, cannot believe their eyes. Were this choice left up to most of us, we would have chosen the strongest, best-looking young man to succeed Saul. It just makes good common sense. Right?

In this contemporary Western culture, image is just about everything. From Facebook, to Instagram, to Twitter, what you look like is often more important than who you are. In a recent study of women's self-image and their use of Facebook, the authors discovered that the mood of women who spend even short amounts of time on Facebook are negatively affected, which agrees, the authors say, with similar research that has been conducted among both men and women.[8] Although image may not be everything, it is one of the main things that we concern ourselves with and that our culture tends to focus on. Even for rabbis of Jesus' day, who they chose as a disciple, or for that matter, to eat with, were important considerations to make. Who was Levi? He was a tax collector. What did people in his culture see? A traitor, a sinner. What did Jesus see? A disciple. What did it mean to answer the call to be a disciple?

---

8. Fardouly et al., "Social Comparisons on Social Media," 21.

Eating with Tax Collectors and Sinners

What Was a Disciple?

In biblical times, a disciple was a student who adhered to the instruction of a teacher.[9] To be a disciple, the one choosing to follow a rabbi needed to be completely devoted to the teaching of the rabbi, becoming like the rabbi by spending time with and listening to him.[10] Though disciples often requested a particular rabbi, rabbis themselves could request disciples.[11] In either case, the rabbi would consider whether the disciple had the potential to follow the rabbi and make the required commitment.[12] Had Levi had the inclination to become a disciple, would the average rabbi have welcomed Levi as a disciple? Absolutely not! Levi was categorized among the tax collectors and sinners. In an amazing, and highly unusual turn of events, Jesus sought out Levi to be a disciple, Levi the tax collector. What did Jesus see in Levi that others did not? In what ways did Jesus consider that Levi had the potential to make a commitment to his teachings?

Luke recounts a parable that Jesus told of a tax collector and a Pharisee in Luke 18:9–14. In the passage, a Pharisee was thanking God that he was not made like others who are evildoers like this tax collector. However, the tax collector who stood apart from the Pharisee cried to God, "Have mercy on me, a sinner" (Luke 18:13, NIV). Jesus told his listeners that the tax collector rather than the Pharisee was justified. Although Pharisees during the time of Jesus were not all self-righteous, Brad Young, in *Jesus the Jewish Theologian*, suggests that Pharisees were highly respected in Jesus' day, even by Jesus himself.[13] In Matthew 23:2–3 (NIV), Jesus informed his hearers to properly respect the position of the Pharisees, "The scribes and the Pharisees sit on Moses' seat; therefore, do whatever they teach you and follow it; but do not do as they do, for they do not practice what they teach." Jesus was probably not speaking of

---

9. Spangler and Tverberg, *Sitting at the Feet of Rabbi Jesus*, 58.
10. Vander Laan, "Rabbi and Talmidim."
11. Vander Laan, "Rabbi and Talmidim."
12. Vander Laan, "Rabbi and Talmidim."
13. Young, *Jesus the Jewish Theologian*, 184.

all Pharisees everywhere, but those that did behave in such a manner. Nonetheless, Luke seems to be portraying Jesus as suggesting something that would have been unusual, out of the ordinary, that in this case the Pharisee was self-righteous and that the tax collector had the appropriate posture before God. Either way, Jesus seemed to have a soft spot for tax collectors, and for that matter, sinners.

Far too often, we likely find ourselves judging sinners as that, sinners. We may say to ourselves, "I'm so glad I'm not like that person, a thief, a liar, a homosexual." We see people like this and make snap judgments that there is no way they can be close to the kingdom of God. All the while not realizing that they may be closer to the kingdom of God than even ourselves in some cases.

It was important that a disciple imitate their rabbi and to follow him closely. A story was told of a disciple who went to considerable lengths to imitate his rabbi. According to the story, he hid in his rabbi's bedroom to learn how to be intimate with his wife in the future.[14] Total commitment. Maybe a bit inappropriate, but still commitment. Possibly this was not the level of imitation that a rabbi expected; nonetheless, imitation was required of his disciple.

After Jesus called Levi to follow him, Levi "left everything and followed him."[15] The disciple was to be totally committed to his rabbi; everything else was secondary.[16] If Levi followed Jesus as disciples followed their rabbis, even Levi's job as a tax collector became secondary at best. As a tax collector, Levi had no Jewish community to go back to; he had no good Jewish friends. He had left his Jewish community in favor of wealth at the expense of his fellow Jews. His own people weren't going to take him into their community. He was shamed and shameful, for all intents and purposes, alone. He only had his occupation and his money. Yet Levi dropped everything and followed Jesus.

As a man living in a Western culture, this level of following and imitating someone else is foreign to me. To leave my job and

---

14. "Being a First-Century Disciple."
15. Luke 5:28 (NIV).
16. Vander Laan, "Rabbi and Talmidim."

my family for a time would be nearly impossible. However, Jesus asked that of Levi, and Levi responded, following Jesus. Are we willing to drop everything to follow our rabbi?

When Zacchaeus, the tax collector, saw Jesus coming into Jericho (Luke 19) Zacchaeus, at Jesus' request, invited Jesus back to his home to stay. While there, Zacchaeus told Jesus that he would give half of his possessions to the poor and four times the amount to everyone he stole from. Now that's a commitment. From what it looks like, Levi didn't respond quite like Zacchaeus; however, Levi expressed his gratitude to Jesus, in part, by inviting him to a banquet.

Jesus at the Banquet of a Sinner

The banquet was not filled with the *upper crust* of the Jewish community. You likely wouldn't find the local Pharisee attending Levi's banquet, nor would you have found an itinerant rabbi. No, Levi invited "tax collectors and others"[17] to the party. Luke softens the blow by saying "others" while the Pharisees and scribes referred to the "others" as "sinners." After all, these were the people that Levi knew and who were willing to get to know him. Do we expect people in our day to leave all that they know, that they are familiar with, who come to know Jesus? Once they *get saved*, they shouldn't be spending time with "sinners" and "others," should they? What did Jesus do? Instead of expecting Levi to leave his friends, Jesus joined Levi and the "others" at a banquet thrown by Levi himself.

This seems like a strange turn of events, particularly if it were to happen today. It's easy to read a Bible passage and be impressed by Jesus' faith and commitment to pursue Levi's friends, the "others" and the "sinners." But when we are expected to do the same, that's simply not going to happen. It was all good for Jesus to pursue the lost; after all, he's the Son of God. It seems to me that Jesus

---

17. Luke 5:29 (NIV).

expects the same from us, that we would "go and make disciples of all nations."[18]

Eating With Sinners

In Jesus' day, to eat with people meant to accept them.[19] To accept them meant that they accepted not just what they did, but who they were. That's not too far off from how society operates today. If your pastor invited the local drunk over to his house for dinner, some people would likely have a problem with that. However, to cause a big stir, it has to become "Facebook Official." If the pastor has his picture taken with the local drunk and posts it on Facebook, that's just going too far. For Jesus, a recognized teacher and rabbi, to accept an invitation of a tax collector to eat with tax collectors would have been seen as deplorable.

One of my responsibilities when I taught undergraduates was teaching "Personal Evangelism." One of the assignments required for the class was for students to engage in some kind of communication with someone they knew or were acquainted with and start a conversation about Jesus and report about it. One young lady in the class asked if she could go to the local bar and witness to people. As an educator at a Christian college that had certain standards that included not going to the bar, I couldn't encourage her consideration. However, together we came up with a compromise: greet people as they left the bar, striking up conversations whenever possible. She did and her report indicated that she was rather successful, in a manner of speaking. A couple of the people who left were somewhat inebriated so the conversations may have been a bit one-sided, but she did visit with them. It was an exciting class period when she shared her experience.

What kind of activity took place at a banquet in first-century Israel? The first-century banquet would have been largely vegetarian as meat was expensive and normally eaten during religious

---

18. Matt 28:19 (NIV).
19. Thacker, "Three Concepts of Tolerance," 67–68.

EATING WITH TAX COLLECTORS AND SINNERS

feasts or very special occasions.[20] The drinks that were common for first-century meals were water and wine.[21] In the story of the wedding at Cana in John 2:1–12, the wedding host was amazed at the wine that Jesus created. At a Jewish wedding in the first century, according to the host, the good wine was brought out first to get the guests drunk, and then the wine of poorer quality was brought out, as the guests would not be aware enough to tell the difference. We aren't told what Levi served at his banquet. Normally, vegetables were main staples at a dinner or even a banquet.[22] When the banquet was intended for a special purpose, possibly a wedding, or a very important guest, meat may have been served.[23] I like to think that as part of Levi's leaving it all behind, he threw a massive feast with all sorts of fruits and vegetables, the choicest meat, and the best wine. Of course, this is only supposition, but one can imagine.

Steve Sjogren tells the story of a pastor friend of his who went to a reggae concert to hear one of his church members play. At a certain time during the event, the pastor went to a concession stand for a carbonated drink when he felt the Lord tell him to buy beer for the next twelve people in line. At this point, many of us would shake our head and walk away from a conversation like this, insisting that Steve's friend could not have heard from God. However, Steve's friend felt the Lord say it was an act of kindness. Many of the people who were there were so shocked that a pastor would do this that several of them attended his church the next day.[24] Should he have done that? Was it wise for him to purchase alcoholic beverages for these people? What would Jesus do?

At this point, I feel it is my obligation to clear a little air. The direction some of this chapter is going makes it appear that I am all for drinking alcohol. I must admit, from a biblical perspective, I don't find any clear argument why not to drink alcohol. I do

20. Neyrcy, "Reader's Guide to Meals."
21. Neyrey, "Reader's Guide to Meals."
22. Neyrey, "Reader's Guide to Meals."
23. Neyrey, "Reader's Guide to Meals."
24. Sjogren et al., *Irresistible Evangelism*, 61–62.

find passages that encourage discipline in drinking alcohol. For instance, in Proverbs 20:1 (NIV) we read, "Wine is a mocker and beer a brawler; whoever is led astray by them is not wise." There you have it, don't drink alcohol, we say. However, in Proverbs 23:20–21 (NIV), we also read, "Do not join those who drink too much wine or gorge themselves on meat, for drunkards and gluttons become poor, and drowsiness clothes them in rage." If I take Proverbs 20:1 (NIV) to mean I can't drink wine, I should take Proverbs 23:20–21 (NIV) to mean I can't eat meat either. But don't you touch my red meat. The point I am making here is that Scripture does not teach not to drink, but not to get drunk, just like it teaches not to become gluttonous. Likely it means more than avoiding gluttony, but also avoiding frivolity. Keep in mind, the typical Jewish meal involved fruits and vegetables. Meat was a rarity. To gorge yourself on meat may have meant not only were you gluttonous, but you were also frivolous by not saving meat for a special occasion likely involving not just yourself but a greater part of the community.

For me, the issue of drinking is not a scriptural one, but a cultural one. I feel that our American culture has a serious problem with discipline and taking some activities to the extreme. For me personally, I am a heavy coffee- and tea-drinker, mostly coffee. I recently made the decision to roast my own coffee. I may have a problem. My wife has teased me that if I were to take up drinking alcohol I would be an alcoholic. Rather, I choose not to drink, partly because my denomination frowns upon it, but also because I feel I would become too dependent on alcohol rather than on the Spirit. And, frankly, I just don't like it. With regard to Jesus, though, the Pharisees were not so objective and thoughtful.

The Pharisees and teachers of the law were shocked: "why do you eat and drink with tax collectors and sinners?"[25] Translation: "Why do you accept these outcasts and sinners, approving of their behavior?" Discovering Jesus with Levi at his banquet would have been similar to you and me discovering our pastor at the local bar with the "sinners" or buying alcohol for several people at a reggae concert. Crazy, right? Notice it was not the presence of wine that

---

25. Luke 5:30 (NIV).

shocked the Pharisees and teachers of the law. It was the presence of tax collectors and sinners; more importantly, it was the presence of Jesus with the tax collectors and the sinners.

Why Were the Pharisees There?

The Pharisees and the teachers of the law questioned Jesus' judgment because of his attendance at a tax collector's banquet; but why were the Pharisees there? Does that seem hypocritical to anyone else? As a tax collector, Levi was wealthy and so likely had an open dwelling layout to his house. The Pharisees, the teachers of the law, and for that matter, nearly anyone could enter and watch as Levi and his tax collector friends partied with Jesus. So, again, why were the Pharisees and teachers of the law there? The passage does not give clear evidence of their motive for observing the party. However, it seems that as Pharisees and teachers of the law, they would be curious, even concerned, about the behavior of Jesus, this so-called rabbi, eating with "tax collectors and sinners,"[26] and possibly wanted to see what Jesus was up to if he was who some people said he was, a great teacher.

It seems that our response as Christians in our Western culture, removed by two thousand years from Jesus' culture, is that we have the tendency to judge the Pharisees unfairly. Possibly, we imagine them huddled together out of reach of some of the "unclean" people in attendance, pointing and sneering at the people Jesus chose to spend his time with. Likely, this is an incorrect perspective of the Pharisees. One of the responsibilities of the Pharisees was to look into claims of messiahship.[27] Were someone to claim to be the messiah, or others claim that this person may be the messiah, the Pharisees would observe and interrogate the subject to determine if he was in fact a candidate for messiahship.[28] Jesus is just beginning to choose disciples, so claims of messiahship

26. Luke 5:30 (NIV).
27. Gallaty, *Forgotten Jesus*, ch. 7.
28. Gallaty, *Forgotten Jesus*, ch. 7.

may not be understood in this scenario. Nonetheless, in later table teachings the Pharisees may be reviewing their messiah checklist with Jesus in mind.

Amy-Jill Levine, in her book, *Short Stories by Jesus: The Enigmatic Parables of a Controversial Rabbi*, indicated that villages had their own Pharisees, rather than Pharisees being based within the temple.[29] Levine suggests that the poor perspective many Christians have of Pharisees today are mostly unfounded; the general view of the Pharisees by the Jews had been predominantly positive, as the Pharisees were the pious representatives of the keepers and teachers of the Torah.[30] If this is the case here, likely the Pharisees are concerned about Jesus' reputation, or simply the purity of the Torah in light of Jesus as a teacher spending time with people who could compromise the teaching of the Torah.

We are a people who seem to thrive on bad news. Or, more accurately, pointing out people, or people groups, who are bad news. Take North American Christians' perspective of Muslims in our country. Qualitatively, I have had several conversations with people who have warned me, or other people I know, to beware of Muslims. Likely, some of this fear is due to the events of 9/11. However, are they all well-founded? Likely not. Just as many have warned me of Muslims, many others have shared stories of positive encounters with Muslims not only in America, but other countries as well. I'm not suggesting that there aren't bad seeds out there. There are bad seeds, but in every people group and every religion. I believe we often like to spread bad news in part because of our fear of engaging with culture, as mentioned in the previous chapter.

The Sick Need a Doctor

Regardless of the Pharisees' motivation for being at Levi's banquet and offering their concern, Jesus' response was brilliant: "It is not the healthy who need a doctor, but the sick. I have not come to call

---

29. Levine, *Short Stories by Jesus*, 192.
30. Levine, *Short Stories by Jesus*, 190.

Eating with Tax Collectors and Sinners

the righteous, but sinners to repentance."[31] Why did Jesus attend the party? Why did he allow himself to be seen by the religious elite at a party with tax collectors and sinners? He was there because the tax collectors and others needed him more than the Pharisees did. Whether the Pharisees were operating in this story out of pious concern or hypocritical distance, they were at least observers of Torah, living in accordance with its regulations and standards. Although Levi was called to be a disciple by Jesus, he was among the group that Jesus said needed a doctor; he and the others were sick, and Jesus was the cure.

The religious needed—and still need—Jesus as much as the sick, i.e., the sinner. So why did Jesus say that? Could it be that the religious know they are healthy, according to their own rules and regulations? Maybe the religious are healthy based on aspects of God's Law, but still lacking in other areas. The sinner and the tax collector know they are sick but in many cases don't know how to get better nor do they have the means to get better. So what did Jesus do? He spent time with them and called one of them to be his disciple. The religious should have done this, but they did not. Whether out of distance or piety, they chose not to be associated with the sick, the sinner.

Let that sink in for a moment. Jesus called someone who needed a doctor, who was sick, who was seen as a sinner to follow him and be his disciple. How would Levi have known how to behave if someone didn't show him? That is where Jesus came into his life and that is where he comes into our lives as well. Do you know people around you who do not yet know Jesus? How will they know unless they see and hear you bring the healing message of Jesus to their life?

Understand here that the Pharisees did not view this as a church vs. the world issue. After all, the people that the Pharisees were offended by were Jews; they were part of the chosen crowd. Rather this was an issue of cleanliness or purity vs. uncleanliness or impurity. The tax collectors and sinners were unclean and impure. As Jesus associated with the unclean and impure, he became

---

31. Luke 5:31–32 (NIV).

Jesus' Table Talk

unclean and impure, so he couldn't be a great teacher, let alone the Messiah figure that some said he was. Or could it be that Jesus took upon himself their uncleanness, their impurity, in exchange for his righteousness and holiness?[32]

The Pharisees and teachers of the law were offended. They were offended that Jesus, a rabbi, would accept the tax collectors and sinners. David Kinnaman and Gabe Lyons, in their book *UnChristian*, stated that Christians have become so sheltered from those who do not believe in Jesus that Christians appear offended to those who do not believe.[33] They probably are not too far from the truth. Jesus was not offended. Rather he recognized that he had a message, a new way of living that the tax collectors and the others, the sinners, needed that the Pharisees and teachers of the Law would not, could not provide. Jesus knew that the tax collectors and the sinners would likely not be in the temple; they would not be in the places where their sin could be accounted for by the ritualistic practices of their religion. Jesus needed to be with them where they were. How else would they hear and see the good news? The Pharisees and the teachers of the law did not approve.

In the early years of youth ministry, during the industrial revolution, as cities were becoming larger and more people were needed to run the big industry machines, churches tried to reach out to the youth. Churches created purity programs that they believed would entice young people away from the filth of the world into the holiness of the church. It didn't work. In fact, youth were enticed more by the world as the church preached that what the world had to offer was bad and what the church had to offer was good. Purity programs are not bad, they're just not that effective. Living purely in a world gone mad, now that's something to take notice of.

Jesus concluded his response to the Pharisees and the teachers of the law by saying:

---

32. Levine, *Short Stories by Jesus*, 153.
33. Kinnaman and Lyons, *UnChristian*, 131.

> No one tears a piece out of a new garment to patch an old one. Otherwise, they will have torn the new garment, and the patch from the new will not match the old. And no one pours new wine into old wineskins. Otherwise, the new wine will burst the skins; the wine will run out and the wineskins will be ruined. No, new wine must be poured into new wineskins. And no one after drinking old wine wants the new, for they say, 'The old is better.'[34]

Wine was made by pressing grapes in a winepress and allowing the fermentation process to begin before pouring the wine into a wine skin. Old wineskins cannot be used to store new wine as the fermentation process would have been too strong, thus rupturing the wine skin. New wine needed new wine skins.[35] Fundamentally, Jesus' new teaching, which was new to the Pharisees and the teachers of the law, would not fit into their framework of thinking, and so needed new wineskins, i.e., new hearts and minds to fill.

Although this teaching was new to the Pharisees, it was not a new teaching. God covenanted with Abraham his intention for Abraham and his offspring, the Israelites and, prominently, Jesus. In Genesis 12:2–3 (NIV), God said to Abraham:

> I will make you into a great nation, and I will bless you;
> I will make your name great, and you will be a blessing.
> I will bless those who bless you, and whoever curses you
> I will curse; and all the peoples on earth will be blessed through you.

Jesus' teaching was from the Torah, God's word. The new teaching, the teaching that the Pharisees were expecting, was not fitting into the old framework. The old teaching, the teaching of the Torah, was better. This may be one reason why the Pharisees of Jesus' day didn't recognize this promise as including all of the world, or that they didn't recognize this promise as including those among the Jewish people who would and should benefit from this promise. Are we so far from this perspective?

---

34. Luke 5:36–39 (NIV).
35. Young, *Jesus the Jewish Theologian*, 158.

In our contemporary, modern church culture, we find ourselves in similar positions to that of the Pharisees. Rather than stepping in with Jesus and providing service and leadership to those who need to be discipled, we stand back, away from the party, from the wine, from what we may think is chaos, and ask, sometimes aloud, "why would anyone choose to hang out with people like that?" We behave much like gnostic Christians, fearing the dirt and the ugly of the world. We behave much like some of the Pharisees that Jesus confronted, desiring to keep ourselves clean to present to God a bride without spot or wrinkle.

It is not by our own efforts, though, that we are free from spot or wrinkle. It is not by avoiding the pain and the sin of the world that we present ourselves clean before God. By doing so, we become the Pharisee that stood apart from the party, obeying our rules but also passing our judgments. All the while, the sick get sicker and the lame become lamer.

As Jesus identified himself as one who had a cure for sickness and lameness, he has also equipped us, his followers, as his residents, his disciples, to address those who are sick and lame and provide them with the antidote.

Questions for Reflection:

1. Jesus called a known tax collector, someone despised by the Jewish community, to be his disciple. If you were Levi, how do you think you would feel?

2. The Pharisees and teachers of the law found Jesus eating with tax collectors and "sinners" and were shocked that he would accept people like that into his life. How would you have responded if you were the Pharisees? Would you have gone to Levi's house for a party? Why? Why not?

Three
The Party Crasher
A Symposium

LUKE 7:36–50 (NIV)

When one of the Pharisees invited Jesus to have dinner with him, he went to the Pharisee's house and reclined at the table. A woman in that town who lived a sinful life learned that Jesus was eating at the Pharisee's house, so she came there with an alabaster jar of perfume. As she stood behind him at his feet weeping, she began to wet his feet with her tears. Then she wiped them with her hair, kissed them and poured perfume on them. When the Pharisee who had invited him saw this, he said to himself, "If this man were a prophet, he would know who is touching him and what kind of woman she is—that she is a sinner." Jesus answered him, "Simon, I have something to tell you." "Tell me, teacher," he said. "Two people owed money to a certain moneylender. One owed him five hundred denarii, and the other fifty. Neither of them had the money to pay him back, so he forgave the debts of both. Now which of them will love him more?" Simon replied, "I suppose the one who had the bigger debt forgiven." "You have judged correctly," Jesus said. Then he turned toward the woman and said to Simon, "Do you see this woman? I came into your house. You did not give me any water for my feet, but she wet my feet with her tears and wiped them with her hair. You did not give me a kiss, but this woman, from the time I entered, has not stopped kissing my feet. You did not put oil on my head, but she has poured perfume on my feet. Therefore, I tell you, her many sins have been forgiven—as her great love has shown. But whoever has been forgiven little loves little." Then Jesus said to her, "Your sins are forgiven." The other guests began to say among themselves, "Who is this who even forgives sins?" Jesus said to the woman, "Your faith has saved you; go in peace."

A FEW YEARS AGO, I had the opportunity to attend a conference held by a particular ecumenical university. Every night of the conference, a symposium was held. The symposium involved dinner, guests, and recognized experts in the field about which we were learning that night. The food was good, the fellowship was pleasant, and the speakers were challenging. There were no unusual happenings, no one barged in, pushing their way to the front of the room to make a spectacle of themselves. As prestigious as these symposia were, I would like to have watched the symposia to which Jesus was invited, particularly this one. In this symposium, Jesus was invited to be the chief honored guest at a meal, a symposium, where he would be the featured expert. Or, was he? However, a party crasher, a woman who kissed Jesus' feet, dripping tears on his feet, and wiping his feet with her hair, interrupted the meal. A scandal to be sure.

Possibly you remember the movie *Pretty Woman* starring Richard Gere and Julia Roberts. Richard Gere played a rich man who brought Julia Roberts, the prostitute, into his world to rescue her from her lifestyle of prostitution. Scenarios were presented of people judging the prostitute for her position in life and the rich man for lowering himself to her position. Being a love story, everything seems to work out in the end. The story of Jesus and the party crasher presents a similar situation where Jesus is judged for lowering himself to a station of sin.

The Party Crasher

Was Jesus the Chief Honored Guest?

The dinner that is taking place fits within a symposium structure, which would have included a host, chief honored guest of notable wisdom or wealth, and other guests.[1] In this case, Jesus would have been the chief honored guest with Simon the Pharisee as the host. The other guests at the table would have been other scribes and Pharisees. One issue though is that if Jesus was invited to be the chief honored guest, why did Simon not greet him properly? The chief honored guest was just that, honored and deserved to be greeted honorably. I will address this further below.

Considering Jesus had several run-ins with Pharisees and scribes up to this point, it seems odd that Pharisees would invite Jesus as a chief honored guest to a symposium. In Luke 5, Jesus identified himself with God, causing the Pharisees present to accuse him of blasphemy. In Luke 6, Jesus and his disciples ate some grain from a field on the Sabbath. The Pharisees questioned Jesus and his disciples, asking why he would do something so unlawful.

We don't know for certain if these are the same Pharisees as were mentioned in Luke 5 and 6; however, could it be that these Pharisees had at least heard about some of the "crazy" things Jesus was doing? Luke informs us that Jesus was in the town called Nain. Up to this point, Jesus' activities had become so prevalent that his exploits were talked about all through Judea. So, whether these Pharisees had direct contact with Jesus or not, they likely at least heard about Jesus, his claims as the Messiah, and what others were saying about him.

Hospitality

In Jesus' day in the Middle East, it was customary for the host to greet people with a kiss, offer them water to wash their feet, and oil to provide refreshment.[2] Hospitality was, and still is, an important quality in the Middle East. Jews look to Abraham as their example

1. See Steele, "Luke 11:37–54."
2. Cosgrove, "A Woman's Unbound Hair," 690–91.

of hospitality.[3] In Genesis 18, when heavenly messengers visited prior to their judgment on Sodom and Gomorrah, Abraham and his wife prepared a feast for them. The feast consisted of bread made from three *seahs* of flour, a choice calf, and cheese curds.[4] According to Lois Tverberg and Ann Spangler in *Sitting at the Feet of Rabbi Jesus*, three *seahs* of flour would have been close to five gallons of flour which would have made a significant amount of bread for these guests.[5] I often find myself wondering what a scene like this would look like today. In our pre-packaged and pre-prepared culture, it would take time to shop for the right cut of beef and the right amount of bread, but no longer than half a day in many cases. In Abraham's day, a feast of these proportions would have taken hours to prepare. No wonder this scene is regarded as a prime example of hospitality.

When my wife and I were first married, we were friends with a married couple that we would spend time with frequently. The time we spent together would be watching TV, eating together, playing games, and more. They were good friends that helped to keep me grounded while I was in Bible college, and kept my wife and I encouraged while we were experiencing newlywed life. One late night after dinner we started playing card games. I was exhausted and had to get up early in the morning for work. After taking a break for a few moments I returned and said, "Well, I think it's time for you two to go home now." My wife was shocked, I was shocked once I realized what I said, but our friends were so understanding, and probably embarrassed, that they left. My host skills left quite a bit to be desired that night.

Possibly the Pharisees invited Jesus to this symposium hoping to figure him out. Were they hoping to convince Jesus to join their team? Possibly they invited Jesus to the symposium to humiliate him. After all, Simon, the host, did not customarily greet Jesus when he came to Simon's house.

3. "Jewish Practices & Rituals."
4. Gen 18:6–8 (NIV).
5. Spangler and Tverberg, *Sitting at the Feet of Rabbi Jesus*, 44.

It seems odd that Simon the Pharisee would neglect to honor the chief honored guest as Jesus entered the house. Withholding a proper greeting could have been a humiliating experience for someone in Jesus' position, though it is possible that Simon intended this to be a challenge to Jesus' honor. However, Halvor Moxnes, in "Honor and Shame," suggests that challenges to honor do not take place among people of different social stations, but similar.[6] That is, if a person during Jesus' day challenged another person of lower social and honor status, the challenger would be dishonored. Honor challenges were common in Jesus' culture.[7] To be confronted by an honor challenge, the one receiving the challenge would need to respond or lose face, which was to lose honor. Likewise, women rarely involved themselves in honor challenges as honor was for a man to defend, not a woman.[8] This will come into play later. If Simon did in fact challenge Jesus' honor by withholding a proper greeting, Jesus would have to be seen as similar to Simon from a social perspective as well as respond to Simon's honor challenge, or lose face socially in the community.

Another theory why Jesus would have been invited to Simon's house as a chief honored guest is found in Robby Gallaty's book, *The Forgotten Jesus: How Western Christians Should Follow an Eastern Rabbi*. Pharisees were responsible for following up on claims of individuals claiming to be the messiah, or that others claimed were the messiah.[9] Of course this is all speculation, but it doesn't seem too far-fetched to consider that the Pharisees and scribes present were checking up on Jesus and some of the claims of his Messiahship.

Although the feast prepared here for Jesus and those present wasn't quite as large as Abraham's feast, it was still an event that required hospitality. Simon had failed to greet Jesus properly. After all, Simon was a Pharisee, someone who was at the least aware of customs of the day and how it might offend someone if those

---

6. Moxnes, "Honor and Shame," 20.
7. Moxnes, "Honor and Shame," 21.
8. Moxnes, "Honor and Shame," 21.
9. Gallaty, *Forgotten Jesus*, 163.

customs were not practiced. Regardless of the reason for not greeting Jesus, the party crasher barged in and greeted Jesus properly, the best she knew how. She wept, anointed Jesus' feet with her tears, wiped his feet with her hair, and kissed his feet.

The Party Crasher

What must have been going through this woman's mind to interrupt a dinner like this? This kind of behavior was not common, and certainly not acceptable in this setting. Symposia were a male-dominated event, at least in the Jewish culture. For a woman to interact so intimately with a member of those present would not have been well-received.

Much like the Pharisees at the banquet Levi hosted, likely the woman was present watching the symposium. At this time, many people in the area and around Judea had heard about Jesus and even encountered him.[10] Possibly she had heard that Jesus was coming and, along with other onlookers, came to see what Jesus might say or do. Possibly she had come to give Jesus a gift, or her intention all along was to crash the party in response to an encounter she had with Christ. Either way, she likely made quite a spectacle.

Being a spectacle isn't always a bad thing. Depending on the context, it can be a positive thing. To be a spectacle on a stage as an actor can be an exciting display of acting ability. To stand on a stage yelling at people present to be quiet may not be a good spectacle. I was a freshman at college and an evening of praise and worship had just concluded. People were milling around, talking and laughing. I felt a bit overwhelmed with God and instead of simply spending some time with him in prayer, I made my way to the stage and yelled at those present to be quiet and leave or get back to praying and worshiping. It sounds spiritual, but it did not serve the purpose I hoped at the time. Thankfully, that only

---

10. Luke 7:17.

happened once. After that, I took to the stage as an actor and made a spectacle of myself in character.

Who was this party crasher? Several opinions about this woman have surfaced throughout the years. Some believe she was a prostitute while others doubted she was a prostitute but agreed that she was incredibly inappropriate, not the least because of her loose hair.[11] Commonly throughout a variety of cultures during the time of Jesus, a woman who left her hair unbound would have had a sexual connotation.[12] The woman was referred to as living "a sinful life."[13] Combining that with her loose hair may provide some insight that she may have been active as a prostitute.

Too many of our Christian leaders have been compromised by living a secretly promiscuous life. Whether the Christian leader was involved in hetero- or homosexual behavior, once they are *found out* their vocation as a minister is usually over, let alone as a trusted leader in the church. Simon's response would not be too different than most of us if we were to see a woman who lived a sinful life barge into a dinner party and proceed to provocatively persuade a respected member of the Christian community.

But wait! Maybe she wasn't a prostitute or at least not a practicing one at this time. In Jesus' day, loose hair did not only suggest sexual promiscuity, but could also refer to the woman as grieving, or even expressing gratitude.[14] If we assume, based on how the woman was reacting with Jesus, that she was reacting with gratitude, that helps to explain her actions as well as Jesus' response. Possibly she had encountered Jesus who offered her forgiveness or healing. Simon's response, "If this man were a prophet, he would know who is touching him and what kind of woman she is—that she is a sinner"[15] also makes sense in that he may have assumed she was behaving overtly sexually.

---

11. Cosgrove, "A Woman's Unbound Hair," 678–86.
12. Cosgrove, "A Woman's Unbound Hair," 678–86.
13. Luke 7:37 (NIV).
14. Cosgrove, "A Woman's Unbound Hair," 678–86.
15. Luke 7:39 (NIV).

In our technologically driven culture it is easy for signals to be crossed. In an SMS, a message is sent that the sender intends to be received one way, but the receiver takes another way and becomes frustrated as a result. In the ubiquity of Facebook, people may post a statement about a particular issue only to have several people deride that person for their own misunderstanding of the statement that person posted. We don't know for sure whether Simon misunderstood the woman's intentions, but we do know that the woman intended to show Jesus the honor she felt he was due.

Jesus, who was aware of Simon's concern, told Simon a parable that should help Simon make sense of the scenario. Jesus presented Simon with two fellows who both owed debts, one larger than the other. They were both forgiven. Jesus asked Simon, who is the more grateful? The one with the larger debt of course.

Jesus the Jubilee

Debt for the Jews in the first century likely represented more than just economic debt, but debt across the entire spectrum of life including spiritual life, physical deficiencies, and others. With regard to this woman, her debt wasn't necessarily financial, but social and spiritual. Jesus introduced to these Pharisees that he has come to address the debt in the life of the Jews that they owed God but could not repay. This debt included their responsibility to be a light to the gentiles, but collectively the Jews failed to be that light. Jesus came to forgive that debt and become for the Jews the light that they were not capable of becoming.[16]

This theme has strong Jubilee references. The Jubilee was announced as a requirement for God's people in Leviticus 25.[17] In this chapter, God commanded that the Israelites celebrate the Jubilee which included several sanctions. The sanctions included a requirement to allow the land to rest for one year, and God will provide the Israelites enough food for three years, the year

---

16. Eisenbaum, *Paul Was Not a Christian*, 253–54.
17. Bruno, "'Jesus is Our Jubilee' . . . But How?," 85.

leading up to the Jubilee, the Jubilee year, and the year after the Jubilee.[18] Redemption of the land was another sanction, with the understanding that if land is sold outside the family it would be returned at the Jubilee.[19] Release of indentured servants, should Israelites fall under another's authority, would ocurr at the year of Jubilee,[20] and if a farmer falls under another's authority outside his family, the family has the right of redemption, and if not possible, the farmer would be released in the year of Jubilee. Israelites were not to be servants of others as they are first servants of Yahweh who redeemed them from Egypt.

The Jubilee year was to take place at the end of every seven times seven years, or every fiftieth year.[21] The Jubilee was intended to set everything right in Israel: slaves would be freed, debts would be canceled, and people and creation would live at rest.[22] Though there is no reference that the year of Jubilee was observed by the Israelites,[23] it is nonetheless a common theme throughout the Old Testament and possibly the New Testament.[24]

During Jesus' time, there were some that believed that there would be a greater Jubilee.[25] Jeremiah, in his prophetic book, Jeremiah 25:12 (NIV), presented a Jubilee promise for God's people while in exile in Babylon: "'But when the seventy years are fulfilled, I will punish the king of Babylon and his nation, the land of the Babylonians, for their guilt,' declares the Lord, 'and will make it desolate forever.'"

Daniel, in Daniel 9:1–3, 20–24 (NIV) asked God when their exile in Babylon will be over. Gabriel appeared before Daniel and responded:

---

18. Bergsma, "Year of Jubilee," 156.
19. Harbin, "Jubilee and Social Justice," 689.
20. Harbin, "Jubilee and Social Justice," 688.
21. Bruno, "'Jesus is Our Jubilee' ... But How?," 85.
22. Lazonby, "Applying the Jubilee," 32–33.
23. Wright, "Theology of Jubilee," 11.
24. Whelan, "Jesus is the Jubilee," 226.
25. Ulrich, "Need for More Attention to Jubilee," 489.

> In the first year of Darius son of Xerxes (a Mede by descent), who was made ruler over the Babylonian kingdom— in the first year of his reign, I, Daniel, understood from the Scriptures, according to the word of the Lord given to Jeremiah the prophet, that the desolation of Jerusalem would last seventy years. So I turned to the Lord God and pleaded with him in prayer and petition, in fasting, and in sackcloth and ashes.
>
> While I was speaking and praying, confessing my sin and the sin of my people Israel and making my request to the Lord my God for his holy hill— while I was still in prayer, Gabriel, the man I had seen in the earlier vision, came to me in swift flight about the time of the evening sacrifice. He instructed me and said to me, "Daniel, I have now come to give you insight and understanding. As soon as you began to pray, a word went out, which I have come to tell you, for you are highly esteemed. Therefore, consider the word and understand the vision:
>
> "Seventy 'sevens' are decreed for your people and your holy city to finish transgression, to put an end to sin, to atone for wickedness, to bring in everlasting righteousness, to seal up vision and prophecy and to anoint the Most Holy Place.

Was the vision that Daniel had and that Jeremiah referred to an actual 490 years? Does the 490 years end on a specific day? Some of these questions are a bit beyond the scope of this book. However, there are some interesting elements to consider.

First, Gabriel announced to Daniel that seventy sevens were decreed for his people to finish transgression. The next time Gabriel is presented is in Luke when he announced the birth of Jesus and John the Baptist.

Second, Matthew began his Gospel with the genealogy of Jesus. When the generations are counted, Matthew lists them in three groups of 14, that's six sevens. Jesus comes at the seventh seven. Matthew 1:17 (NIV) says, "All those listed above include fourteen generations from Abraham to David, fourteen from David to the Babylonian exile, and fourteen from the Babylonian exile to the Messiah." It appears that Matthew is referring to the appearance of Jesus as the "Jubilee of Jubilees."[26]

In Isaiah 61:1–2 (NIV), Isaiah wrote:

> The Spirit of the Sovereign Lord is on me, because the Lord has anointed me to proclaim good news to the poor. He has sent me to bind up the brokenhearted, to proclaim freedom for the captives and release from darkness for the prisoners, to proclaim the year of the Lord's favor.

In Luke 4, Jesus went to the synagogue on the Sabbath and a scroll was handed to him to read. The scroll contained this passage from Isaiah. It is believed that this passage referred to the Jubilee.[27] After reading this passage, Jesus sat down and said to those listening, "Today this scripture is fulfilled in your hearing."[28] If the Isaiah passage refers to the Jubilee, and Jesus announced that this passage has been fulfilled, what would the first-century Jew listening to Jesus at this time be thinking? Likely, that Jesus was the fulfillment of the Jubilee.[29]

The Party Crasher, the True Host?

Apparently this woman had lived a sinful life, but had responded to Jesus' Jubilee of love and offer of forgiveness and so responded to Jesus in an overtly thankful way. So this woman, more than Simon, responded to Jesus as Simon the host should have, by kissing him, giving him water to refresh his feet and oil for his hair. Simon failed to be a loving and gracious host and Jesus called him on it. Likely, Simon intentionally neglected to appropriately welcome Jesus. This woman experienced much by way of love and forgiveness and so became to Jesus the true host.

---

26. Ulrich, "Need for More Attention to Jubilee," 489.
27. Wright, "Theology of Jubilee," 16.
28. Luke 4:21 (NIV).
29. Wright, "Theology of Jubilee," 16.

Interestingly, Jesus acknowledged to Simon that more than he, this woman was the proper host because she greeted him properly. If in fact Simon's neglect to greet Jesus was an honor challenge, it appears as if Jesus may have won the challenge. Jesus not only acknowledged that Simon did not greet him properly, but asserted that the woman greeted him when Simon the host failed to. Here, Jesus not only retains his honor, but acknowledged that a woman functioned more properly as a host than Simon the Pharisee, thus dishonoring Simon. So, in retaining his own honor, Jesus also gave honor to the woman: a true sign of love and compassion.

How do we come to terms with that? If Jesus did in fact win an honor challenge, doesn't that seem less Christ-like than we often assume Christ-likeness should look like? In other words, that wasn't very nice, was it? We must take into account that women were not part of honor challenges.[30] In spite of that, Jesus involved the woman in the honor challenge by acknowledging that she, not Simon, was the proper host, thus shaming Simon. While shaming Simon, though, Jesus honored the woman, the true host. Regardless of her station in life, regardless of her gender, this woman demonstrated honor to whom honor was due, Jesus. In the exchange, Simon lost some of his honor and the woman gained honor. How does that translate in our culture?

In Jesus' day, women were not necessarily second-class humans, but they also were not equal to men in public authority.[31] Though women were not socially equal to men, they also weren't necessarily considered as inferior.[32] Interestingly, the issue of male dominance and female inferiority were less a part of the culture in Jesus' day than we today often think it was.[33] It seems that the common perspective by many today, particularly women, is that women of Jesus' day were underprivileged, seen as less than human, had little or no rights, and were baby factories. Although this was not always the case, we also shouldn't assume that everything

---

30. Moxnes, "Honor and Shame," 21.
31. Frymer-Kensky, *Reading the Women of the Bible*, xvi.
32. Frymer-Kensky, *Reading the Women of the Bible*, xvi.
33. Frymer-Kensky, *Reading the Women of the Bible*, xvi.

was smooth sailing for women either. The bottom line is that women, though not inferior, were not seen as social equals in several settings.

As the woman in our story showed honor to Jesus, and in turn, Jesus showed honor to her by regarding her as the true host, lessons were taught that we in our culture would be wise to learn. First, Jesus elevated this woman in the story to that of host, seemingly above Simon, the male authority in the household. When Simon failed to show proper hospitality, this woman became the true host. There are plenty of people around us we may assume are not deserving of honor or respect. Possibly we act as if they aren't there, someone to ignore, or worse, we disrespect them for their assumed position in society. Facebook seems to bring to light the true feeling of people in relation to others' opinions and perspectives. When a controversial comment is posted, one that Christians often disagree with, some of the posts by those espousing a Christian allegiance will be anything but respectful. Granted some of the people that we disagree with may hold very different opinions to ours, but does that give us the right as Christ followers to badger, belittle, and berate them in a semi-public forum like Facebook? This kind of behavior becomes dishonoring to Jesus as we dishonor others who need to see the light of Christ exhibited in our monologues and dialogues.

Second, in spite of this woman's perceived social status, whether prostitute or former prostitute, Jesus didn't shun her or turn her away, as Simon expected him to. Instead of shunning this woman, Jesus honored her for her unexpected hospitality. Did Jesus honor her because of the hospitality she showed to him? Possibly. Though, I believe he would have honored her had she demonstrated hospitality to anyone else in the face of Simon choosing not to demonstrate hospitality. To whom do you show hospitality? To people you believe deserve it? To your friends and family? Or, do you show hospitality to anyone in need, even if they are deemed by others to be undeserving of hospitality?

Image of Love

The woman had let her hair down and Simon saw someone undeserving of attention, let alone a place at the table. The woman was not concerned about who saw her or what others at the table thought of her, she was desperate to greet Jesus and demonstrate her love and thankfulness. Perhaps you recall the scene in 2 Samuel 6 when David was dancing as the ark of the covenant was returning to Jerusalem. Michal, David's wife, saw him and said, frustrated and embarrassed, "How the king of Israel has distinguished himself today, going around half-naked in full view of the slave girls of his servants as any vulgar fellow would."[34] David responded, "I will become even more undignified than this, and I will be humiliated in my own eyes."[35] It wasn't dignity or propriety that concerned David, or for that matter, this woman at Jesus' feet. Rather it was honor and love that drove them to be undignified.

The woman was more than a prostitute, more than the image that others had associated her with, but Simon did not see that. Rather he felt it was important for Jesus as the good rabbi, or even the Messiah, to kick this prostitute out. Jesus, on the other hand, did not see a prostitute but a human being in need of love and forgiveness. It is too easy for us to consider people by their social stigmas, by how they have treated us, or by how culture views them. Jesus demonstrated time and again that he was not concerned with societal stigmas, boundaries, or traditions. Rather, Jesus was concerned about the woman who needed love and forgiveness and she was granted that by her new rabbi, Jesus. Like Jesus, we need to be willing to allow people to *let their hair down* around us, but first we need to be the kind of people, like Jesus, who people like this woman would feel safe with, the kind of people who may seem a bit undignified but are truly worshiping our Lord and Savior.

In his letter to Philemon, Paul addressed Philemon, a member of the Colossian church, or possibly a house church leader in Colosse. Philemon's slave, Onesimus, stole from Philemon and ran

---

34. 2 Sam 6:20 (NIV).
35. 2 Samuel 6:22 (NIV).

away. Apparently, Onesimus happened to meet Paul, a prisoner, who introduced Onesimus to Jesus. As a new brother in Christ, Paul felt compelled to write to Philemon about Onesimus's anticpated return to Colosse, and appealed to Philemon's character when he said in verse 7, "Your love has given me great joy and encouragement, because you, brother, have refreshed the hearts of the Lord's people."[36] What Paul is saying is, "Philemon, you're a good person, you're the kind of person other people love to be around, now refresh the heart of Onesimus, your new brother in Christ." Apparently, Philemon did so. In fact, as legend has it, Philemon released Onesimus from his service and Onesimus went on to become the Bishop of Ephesus, where he was martyred for Christ. Onesimus the slave, the thief, became Onesimus the bishop, church leader of Ephesus.

Labels can be helpful, but labels can also be hurtful and even destructive. When the person at the clinic carries the label of doctor, you may find yourself more at ease hearing the prognosis and how to correct your malady. When the person you are watching carries the label of athlete, you may find yourself excited to watch someone so gifted do things you only wish you could do.

When someone carries with them the label of prostitute, ugly, stupid, or a multitude of other derogatory labels, often as the church and followers of Jesus we find ourselves less likely to spend time with them. However, those are the very people Jesus wants us to spend time with.

In the story of Gideon in Judges 6–7, Gideon was found by an angel of the Lord hiding on the threshing floor, away from the Midianites. The angel appeared to Gideon and called him "mighty warrior."[37] How much more confusing could a label like that be? Gideon was anything but mighty and definitely not a warrior. After some persuading, Gideon tore down the Asherah pole on his father's property as instructed by God. The men in the city found

---

36. Phlm 7 (NIV).
37. Judg 6:12 (NIV).

out and labeled Gideon Jerub-Baal, that is, "Let Baal contend with him."[38]

In chapter 7, the narrator says the following, "Early in the morning, Jerub-Baal (that is, Gideon)..."[39] In this part of the story the narrator uses the label that the men in Gideon's town labeled him with and reminded the reader that though Gideon is labeled as defeated by his own townspeople, God has labeled him Gideon, "mighty warrior." As the story continues, Gideon contended with Baal and, with God's help, won the victory for his people. Baal contended with Gideon, but Gideon, with God on his side, won the victory.

There are likely many mighty warriors around us. Do we label them as losers, as lost, as hopeless? Or, like Jesus, do we label them as disciples, as worthy, as conquerors, as mighty warriors?

Questions for Reflection:

1. How do you view people that are different than you, or even presumably more "sinful" than you?
2. Are you willing to let someone "let their hair down" around you and ask for your help?
3. Do you feel like you are a safe person that people can come to about their problems?

---

38. Judg 6:32 (NIV).
39. Judg 7:1 (NIV).

Four
The One with the Woes
A Symposium

LUKE 11:37-54 (NIV)

When Jesus had finished speaking, a Pharisee invited him to eat with him; so he went in and reclined at the table. But the Pharisee was surprised when he noticed that Jesus did not first wash before the meal. Then the Lord said to him, "Now then, you Pharisees clean the outside of the cup and dish, but inside you are full of greed and wickedness. You foolish people! Did not the one who made the outside make the inside also? But now as for what is inside you—be generous to the poor, and everything will be clean for you. "Woe to you Pharisees, because you give God a tenth of your mint, rue and all other kinds of garden herbs, but you neglect justice and the love of God. You should have practiced the latter without leaving the former undone. "Woe to you Pharisees, because you love the most important seats in the synagogues and respectful greetings in the marketplaces. "Woe to you, because you are like unmarked graves, which people walk over without knowing it." One of the experts in the law answered him, "Teacher, when you say these things, you insult us also." Jesus replied, "And you experts in the law, woe to you, because you load people down with burdens they can hardly carry, and you yourselves will not lift one finger to help them. "Woe to you, because you build

Jesus' Table Talk

tombs for the prophets, and it was your ancestors who killed them. So you testify that you approve of what your ancestors did; they killed the prophets, and you build their tombs. Because of this, God in his wisdom said, 'I will send them prophets and apostles, some of whom they will kill and others they will persecute.' Therefore this generation will be held responsible for the blood of all the prophets that has been shed since the beginning of the world, from the blood of Abel to the blood of Zechariah, who was killed between the altar and the sanctuary. Yes, I tell you, this generation will be held responsible for it all. "Woe to you experts in the law, because you have taken away the key to knowledge. You yourselves have not entered, and you have hindered those who were entering." When Jesus went outside, the Pharisees and the teachers of the law began to oppose him fiercely and to besiege him with questions, waiting to catch him in something he might say.

DID SOMETHING SET JESUS off? Jesus appears to have gone on a bit of a verbal rampage in this passage. Luke wrote that "when Jesus had finished speaking, a Pharisee invited him to eat with him."[1] But what had Jesus just finished speaking?

At the beginning of Luke 11, a disciple asked Jesus to teach him to pray.[2] The events of Jesus teaching his disciples to pray seem to take place at a different time from the events of Luke 11:14 to the end of the chapter. At verse 14, Jesus drove out a demon from a man. Soon after, the crowd began to accuse Jesus of being in alignment with Beelzebul. At this point, Jesus began a series of lessons beginning with the lesson of who really sent him in contrast to who his accusers were in alignment with. Jesus could not be driving out demons in the name of Satan, "If Satan is divided against himself, how can his kingdom stand?"[3] Jesus emphasized that it

---

1. Luke 11:37 (NIV).
2. Luke 11:1.
3. Luke 11:19 (NIV).

was "by the finger of God"[4] that he drove out demons, indicating that the kingdom of God had come upon them.

After this lesson, Jesus moved directly into accusing those listening of being wicked, for though they demanded a sign, they wouldn't believe it.[5] The sign they would be given, Jesus said, was that of Jonah preaching to the Ninevites.[6] Whereas the Ninevites responded, this generation to whom Jesus was speaking would be condemned for their unbelief.

Finally, Jesus reminded those listening that they needed to have a good eye, an eye filled with light.[7] The lesson to have a good eye, or a healthy eye was a Jewish idiom for having an eye that saw the needs of others and responded to meet their needs.[8] If your eye is good or healthy, you are likely to see the needs of others and help them. In contrast, if your eye is bad, dark, or unhealthy, you are unlikely to see the needs of others, or if you do, you are unlikely to do anything about it.[9] It is interesting that just after this lesson, Jesus was invited to a Pharisee's house and began to unload on the Pharisees and scribes present for their lack of concern for and for heaping burdens on others; in other words, they had bad eyes.

What Frustrated Jesus?

If these teachings of Jesus are read from one perspective, it almost sounds like Jesus is becoming increasingly frustrated. Jesus was known for teaching about a way of life that was different than many were familiar with in that culture. Jesus' teaching was not about how to have power and authority in an age when power and authority belonged to Rome. Jesus' teaching was about the kingdom of heaven coming to earth and how he and his followers would

4. Luke 11:20 (NIV).
5. Luke 11:29.
6. Luke 11:30.
7. Luke 11:34.
8. Tverberg, *Walking in the Dust of Rabbi Jesus*, 69.
9. Tverberg, *Walking in the Dust of Rabbi Jesus*, 70.

serve as they ushered in the new kingdom rather than bring about the new kingdom by force. Jesus probably was a bit frustrated, particularly at the Pharisees and the scribes. So when the Pharisee is surprised that Jesus did not wash his hands ceremoniously before the meal, Jesus turned on his hosts.

Another gospel passage may be of use in helping to understand what Jesus was angry about. Mark 7:1-8 (NIV):

> The Pharisees and some of the teachers of the law who had come from Jerusalem gathered around Jesus and saw some of his disciples eating food with hands that were defiled, that is, unwashed. (The Pharisees and all the Jews do not eat unless they give their hands a ceremonial washing, holding to the tradition of the elders. When they come from the marketplace they do not eat unless they wash. And they observe many other traditions, such as the washing of cups, pitchers and kettles.) So the Pharisees and teachers of the law asked Jesus, "Why don't your disciples live according to the tradition of the elders instead of eating their food with defiled hands?" He replied, "Isaiah was right when he prophesied about you hypocrites; as it is written: "'These people honor me with their lips, but their hearts are far from me. They worship me in vain; their teachings are merely human rules.' You have let go of the commands of God and are holding on to human traditions."

In the Mark passage, Jesus made it clear that these Pharisees were more concerned with outward appearance and looking pure than following the commands of God and being pure. They were more concerned with outward appearance than inward transformation. They were more concerned with observing the traditions of the elders rather than keeping the Law of Moses, that is, to love your neighbor and love God. In the Luke passage, Jesus again turned on the Pharisees and scribes for their hypocrisy and concern about image and tradition of man more than about righteousness and justice.

In Exodus 30:17-21, God commanded Aaron and his descendants, the priests who ministered in the temple, to wash their hands prior to temple ministry. The ritual of washing hands, during Jesus' time, was likely developed as part of rabbinic instruction. While the person washed his hands he would recite a blessing. The blessing would likely have been, "Blessed is he who has sanctified us with thy commandments, and commanded us about washing our hands."[10] If the person neglected to wash his hands, this was seen as a great transgression. So the Pharisees and scribes were likely not just surprised but offended that Jesus didn't wash his hands before dinner.

The Oral Law

Jesus has never been one to be overly impressed by image. In Mark 12:41–44, Jesus and his disciples were sitting outside the temple watching as people put their temple offering into the treasury. Matthew pointed out that the rich were dropping their coins into the treasury. Often the rich would do this to make a spectacle of themselves; the louder the clang, the more it sounded like they gave. However, as a poor widow drops a small amount into the treasury, Jesus instructs his disciples that this widow gave more than the rich: "They all gave out of their wealth; but she, out of her poverty, put in everything—all she had to live on."[11]

So why did Jesus become so aggravated when the Pharisee pointed out that he hadn't washed his hands? In Exodus 30:20 (NIV), we read:

> Whenever they [Aaron and his sons] enter the tent of meeting, they shall wash with water so that they will not die. Also, when they approach the altar to minister by presenting a food offering to the Lord, they shall wash their hands and feet so that they will not die. This is to be a lasting ordinance for Aaron and his descendants for the generations to come.

---

10. "Meal Hand-Washing."
11. Mark 12:44 (NIV).

The command to wash hands was given to Aaron and his sons, the priests alone. The tradition to wash hands before eating was not a command given by God, but instructions in the Oral Law.[12] The Oral Law is not divine command but tradition. Jesus' problem was that the Pharisees placed tradition at the level of the Torah.

Tradition is not a bad thing. Tradition can help to connect us to our past, to our church, to our families, to our community, ultimately to Jesus. However, when we view tradition at the level of God's word, we may find ourselves in danger of siding with tradition rather than siding with what God has commanded. Regarding tradition, Jesus quoted Isaiah 29:13 in Mark 7:6–8 (NIV) when he said, "Isaiah was right when he prophesied about you hypocrites; as it is written: 'These people honor me with their lips, but their hearts are far from me. They worship me in vain; their teachings are merely human rules.' You have let go of the commands of God and are holding on to human traditions." The problem was not necessarily the washing of hands, but the hearts of the Pharisees at the neglect of the Torah and of a right relationship with God and with others.

In Jesus' day a particular practice referred to as "Stringing Pearls" was common.[13] Stringing pearls involved a teacher, like Jesus, making reference to a passage of Scripture that his listeners would have been familiar with, while implying the larger context of the passage. In this case, Jesus referred to one small verse from Isaiah that when the larger context is regarded, a fuller picture comes into view. The larger context of Isaiah 29 (NIV), particularly verses 11–16, says:

> For you this whole vision is nothing but words sealed in a scroll. And if you give the scroll to someone who can read, and say, "Read this, please," they will answer, "I can't; it is sealed." Or if you give the scroll to someone who cannot read, and say, "Read this, please," they will answer, "I don't know how to read." The Lord says: 'These people come near to me with their mouth and honor me with their lips, but their hearts are far from me. Their

---

12. Lipnick, "Did Jesus Neglect to Wash His Hands Before Supper?"
13. Spangler and Tverberg, *Sitting at the Feet of Rabbi Jesus*, 38.

worship of me is based on merely human rules they have been taught. Therefore once more I will astound these people with wonder upon wonder; the wisdom of the wise will perish, the intelligence of the intelligent will vanish.' Woe to those who go to great depths to hide their plans from the Lord, who do their work in darkness and think, 'Who sees us? Who will know?' You turn things upside down, as if the potter were thought to be like the clay! Shall what is formed say to the one who formed it, 'You did not make me'? Can the pot say to the potter, 'You know nothing'?

By referencing this passage in Isaiah, Jesus appears to be confronting the Pharisees and scribes present with their own pride and arrogance. They know what God's word says but they do not do what it says; they refuse to read it. They are like a pot saying to its creator, *you don't know what you're doing!* Which in the end is entirely incomprehensible. In referencing this passage in regards to the Pharisees and scribes present, Jesus was offering a scathing commentary on their hearts in relationship to God and the people.

A Right Perspective

Paul gave the Roman church an interesting instruction. In Romans 14, Paul offered instruction to the Jewish and Roman believers in Rome to be patient with one another's faith expression. Some believers ate meat sacrificed to idols while others did not. Some believers considered one day special while others did not. Paul encouraged the two groups of people, Jews and gentiles, to exercise love with one another. Paul concluded his lesson by saying,

Therefore let us stop passing judgment on one another. Instead, make up your mind not to put any stumbling block or obstacle in the way of a brother or sister. I am convinced, being fully persuaded in the Lord Jesus, that nothing is unclean in itself. But if anyone regards something as unclean, then for that person it is unclean. If your brother or sister is distressed because of what you eat, you are no longer acting in love. Do not by your eating destroy someone for whom Christ died. Therefore do not let what you know is good be spoken of as evil. For the kingdom of God is not a matter of eating and drinking, but of righteousness, peace and joy in the Holy Spirit, because anyone who serves Christ in this way is pleasing to God and receives human approval. Let us therefore make every effort to do what leads to peace and to mutual edification.[14]

Paul instructed his readers, including you and me, that some people hold to tradition and some people do not. Some people consider certain days as more holy than others, while other people may not share the same conviction. The bottom line is, according to Paul, that despite our differences of opinion, the community of believers should be motivated by love and mutual edification. The Pharisees in this story did not share the same sentiment about Jesus' lack of regard for washing his hands.

The Real Issue

To be fair, the Pharisees and scribes, in most cases, believed they were doing the right thing. They believed that their faithfulness to what they thought was the Law was what made them righteous. They were the images of true devotion that every other Jew should follow. So, when Jesus confronted the Pharisees and scribes who were offended that Jesus did not wash his hands, they were perplexed.

Jesus delivered a series of three woes to the Pharisees and to the scribes. The theme of the woes toward the Pharisees included:

1. Neglect of justice and love;
2. Pride;
3. Unmarked graves.

The theme of the woes toward the scribes included:

1. Burdening others with practice;

14. Rom 14:13–19 (NIV).

2. Responsible for the death of the prophets;
3. Taking away key knowledge.

Jesus' woes delivered to the Pharisees centered on their hypocrisy, their concern about image over justice and love. Jesus' woes delivered to the scribes centered on undue burdens that were not from God that they placed on the people. Rather by placing undue burdens on the people, the scribes removed the people's access to God through their own development of and authority over Scripture.

To the Pharisees, Jesus' accusations centered on them neglecting a right relationship with others, or in other words not concerning themselves with the plight of their neighbors and so not demonstrating love. He accused them of avarice, pride, and regarding themselves greater than others. Jesus accused them of looking good on the outside but ultimately having no more than death on the inside.

To the scribes, Jesus' accusations centered on them placing burdens on others from their own traditions that were too difficult and unnecessary for others to bear. He accused the scribes and their prideful protection of their own traditions as being what ultimately cost the prophets their lives. Jesus accused them of withholding the knowledge of Scripture from the people as if they alone were the purveyors of truth.

Who were the Scribes?

The scribes of Jesus' day were the experts in the Torah, the teachers of the law.[15] The scribes worked alongside the Pharisees[16] though they were, in a sense, the teachers of the law that the Pharisees lived by.[17] As such, the scribes were the primary authority of the Torah. Schams says of the development of the scribes:

---

15. Schams, *Jewish Scribes in the Second-Temple Period*, 17.
16. Wellhausen, *Pharisees and Sadducees*, 6.
17. Schams, *Jewish Scribes in the Second-Temple Period*, 17.

[I]n the Hellenistic period a class of lay experts in the Scriptures gradually gained importance and influence alongside the traditional experts, guardians and teachers of the Torah, namely the priests. This development was supposedly caused by the rise in importance of the Scriptures in popular estimation and a general need for legal experts in society.[18]

The scribes' primary concern was the recognized authority of the Law, though as a result, the scribes became dominant in the Jewish culture.[19] The authority of the scribes was much like that of a school master over his students, the school master being the scribes and the students being the Jewish people, including the Pharisees.[20] The scribes were the teachers of the law for the whole of Israel.[21]

Who were the Pharisees?

The Pharisees were the primary students of the scribes.[22] In essence, the Pharisees were regarded as "true Israel."[23] When Pharisees were thought of, the idea of *righteousness* would have come to mind.[24] As a religious sect, they separated themselves out from the rest of the Jews, the weak and incapable of living truly according to the Torah.[25] So, the Pharisees were a zealous group, living with a singular mind according to the teachings of the scribes, living rightly and holy by the standards for the Jewish people.[26] Because of their righteous living, they were the moral correction officers

---

18. Schams, *Jewish Scribes in the Second Temple Period*, 17.
19. Wellhausen, *Pharisees and Sadducees*, 11.
20. Wellhausen, *Pharisees and Sadducees*, 12.
21. Wellhausen, *Pharisees and Sadducees*, 13.
22. Wellhausen, *Pharisees and Sadducees*, 15.
23. Wellhausen, *Pharisees and Sadducees*, 13.
24. Wellhausen, *Pharisees and Sadducees*, 13.
25. Wellhausen, *Pharisees and Sadducees*, 14.
26. Wellhausen, *Pharisees and the Sadducees*, 15.

among the Jews.[27] In spite of their corrective behavior and zealousness of living out the Law, they were highly regarded among the Jewish people.[28] Young says of the perspective of the Jewish people and the Pharisees, "The original audience listening to the story did not consider the Pharisee to be a stereotype of the self-righteous hypocrite. On the contrary, the Pharisees were respected for their sincere piety."[29] Young goes on to suggest that the popular opinion of Pharisees held by the average Jew was not that Pharisees were hypocrites or overzealous overlords of the Torah, rather they were respected and revered precisely because of their piety.[30]

Jesus the Rabbi

Enter Jesus . . . Jesus was not opposed to Pharisees or scribes in general. They had a lot in common. They were both concerned about properly interpreting and demonstrating the law. Depending on which group of Pharisees Jesus was compared with, for instance the Pharisees who belonged to the house of Hillel, a more liberal understanding of Scripture was taken, whereas the Shammai were far more stringent.[31] One of the major disagreements was on the time Jesus spent with sinners and tax collectors. So, would Jesus have been associated more with the house of Shammai or of the house of Hillel? How about you?

Was Jesus a Pharisee or a scribe? Reading through the Gospels, you can certainly see how Jesus could have been regarded as a Pharisee, living according to the Torah. Likewise, you can see how he may have been regarded as a scribe, interpreting the Torah for himself and for his followers. Jesus was from an ordinary family, not directly associated with the priestly class, so likely Jesus

---

27. Wellhausen, *Pharisees and the Sadducees*, 16.
28. Wellhausen, *Pharisees and the Sudducees*, 16.
29. Young, *Jesus the Jewish Theologian*, 183.
30. Young, *Jesus the Jewish Theologian*, 184.
31. Falk, *Jesus the Pharisee*, 24.

was not considered a scribe or a Pharisee.[32] Jesus began his life as a mason's son, learning the trade of his father, Joseph. In Jesus' ministry, he provided interpretations of the Torah (Matt 5–7) and told parables, much like a rabbi.[33] Also, Jesus called for himself disciples who studied under and with him for years, another typical mark of a rabbi.[34] One of the marks of a rabbi was his view of debate.[35] Good debate brings a person closer to the truth rather than draws them further away, according to Jewish teaching.[36] And Jesus enjoyed a good debate as exemplified by this passage in Luke.

Love Your Neighbor

As the religious leaders of the Jewish people, the Pharisees and the scribes represented the failure of the Jewish people to fulfill the promise made to Abraham that his seed would be a blessing to the whole world.[37]

With this sense of separation, legalism, and religious bondage from the scribes and some sects of the Pharisees, new light can be shed on the woes Jesus delivered in this symposium. Jesus saw that the scribes and Pharisees were keeping people from God. The very people who should lead others to God were establishing laws and rules to keep people away.

The meaning of the Torah was not to add burdens, and certainly not to keep people from God, but to demonstrate love: love for God and love for their neighbors. But what does love look like that reflects the Torah, and who would be our neighbor?

Jesus said that the Law and the prophets hang on the point about love for God and love for neighbor (Matt 22:38–40). How does not working your oxen or servants on the Sabbath, not

---

32. Spangler and Tverberg, *Sitting at the Feet of Rabbi Jesus*, 33.
33. Spangler and Tverberg, *Sitting at the Feet of Rabbi Jesus*, 31.
34. Spangler and Tverberg, *Sitting at the Feet of Rabbi Jesus*, 38.
35. Spangler and Tverberg, *Sitting at the Feet of Rabbi Jesus*, 33.
36. Spangler and Tverberg, *Sitting at the Feet of Rabbi Jesus*, 33.
37. Eisenbaum, *Paul Was Not a Christian*, 253–54.

harvesting the corners of your field, honoring God during harvest festivals, and many more commands in the Torah, relate to loving God and loving your neighbor? These laws demonstrated concrete examples of what loving your neighbor and loving your God must look like. God is not interested only in his people following rules but living out the meaning of the rules in concrete, real ways as was instructed in the Law to care for all of creation, humanity and nature included.[38]

When Jesus laid into the Pharisees and scribes, he accused them not only of not loving their neighbor, but in fact of doing harm to their neighbor. In Luke 10:30–37, Jesus told the story of the Samaritan caring for the Jew on the road to Jericho. Jesus didn't say that the Levite and the priest were unfaithful to God, but they were not faithful to their neighbor. If we learn anything from Jesus, we learn that if we are unfaithful in one part of the Torah, we are unfaithful in all of it. The priest and Levite were unfaithful in caring for their neighbor. Instead, a Samaritan became the hero of the story. The Samaritan, the enemy of the Jew, became the hero to the Jew, his own enemy.[39] Jesus' point in the story of the Samaritan was to remind his listeners that not only those we consider friends but also those we consider enemies are our neighbors. That put a whole new spin on things for many of the Jews listening to Jesus' parable of the Samaritan, including the Pharisees and scribes.

Where Israel failed, where the leadership in Israel failed, it was a Samaritan, a hated person by the Jew, who saved the day. By providing a demonstration of how the Samaritan cared for the Jew, Jesus encouraged his hearers to do likewise. Rather than simply say that you are loving, or say that you want to be a more loving person, demonstrate love to people in concrete, active ways that mean something to the real needs of real people.

In our compartmentalized Western culture, it is easy for us to say we love our neighbor but do nothing to actually demonstrate that love. It is easy for us to say we love God but do nothing

---

38. Fung, "Sabbath," 322.
39. Young, *Jesus the Jewish Theologian*, 169.

to actually demonstrate our love for God. James wrote in James 2:20-24 (NIV):

> You foolish person, do you want evidence that faith without deeds is useless? Was not our father Abraham considered righteous for what he did when he offered his son Isaac on the altar? You see that his faith and his actions were working together, and his faith was made complete by what he did. And the scripture was fulfilled that says, 'Abraham believed God, and it was credited to him as righteousness,' and he was called God's friend. You see that a person is considered righteous by what they do and not by faith alone.

How do we show our love to our neighbors? Not just the people we like, but our own enemies? The Muslim across the street, the homosexual couple living next to you, the vindictive agnostic angry at you and the church? How do you demonstrate your love for those people? Faith should be accompanied by actions. The Pharisees and scribes that Jesus confronted were concerned with actions but not faith. Often today we find ourselves concerned about faith and not actions. Jesus would say faith and actions must live together. Not simply in balance, but as one being praising the Lord and loving our neighbors.

Questions for Reflection:

1. What expectations do you have of yourself and/or of others when it comes to God's word and traditions?
2. God's word is meant to free us from burdens not add them. How do you help others to be free from burdens in your own life and ministry?
3. How do you demonstrate love for your neighbor, your community, and your environment?

Five

The Seat of Humility

A Symposium

LUKE 14:1-24 (NIV)

One Sabbath, when Jesus went to eat in the house of a prominent Pharisee, he was being carefully watched. There in front of him was a man suffering from abnormal swelling of his body. Jesus asked the Pharisees and experts in the law, "Is it lawful to heal on the Sabbath or not?" But they remained silent. So taking hold of the man, he healed him and sent him on his way. Then he asked them, "If one of you has a child or an ox that falls into a well on the Sabbath day, will you not immediately pull it out?" And they had nothing to say.

When he noticed how the guests picked the places of honor at the table, he told them this parable: "When someone invites you to a wedding feast, do not take the place of honor, for a person more distinguished than you may have been invited. If so, the host who invited both of you will come and say to you, 'Give this person your seat.' Then, humiliated, you will have to take the least important place. But when you are invited, take the lowest place, so that when your host comes, he will say to you, 'Friend, move up to a better place.' Then you will be honored in the presence of all the other guests. For all those who exalt themselves will be humbled, and those who humble themselves will be exalted."

Then Jesus said to his host, "When you give a luncheon or dinner, do not invite your friends, your brothers or sisters, your relatives, or your rich neighbors; if you do, they may invite you back and so you will be repaid. But when you give a banquet, invite the poor, the crippled, the lame, the blind, and you will be blessed. Although they cannot repay you, you will be repaid at the resurrection of the righteous."

When one of those at the table with him heard this, he said to Jesus, "Blessed is the one who will eat at the feast in the kingdom of God." Jesus replied: "A certain man was preparing a great banquet and invited many guests. At the time of the banquet he sent his servant to tell those who had been invited, 'Come, for everything is now ready.' "But they all alike began to make excuses. The first said, 'I have just bought a field, and I must go and see it. Please excuse me.' "Another said, 'I have just bought five yoke of oxen, and I'm on my way to try them out. Please excuse me.' "Still another said, 'I just got married, so I can't come.' "The servant came back and reported this to his master. Then the owner of the house became angry and ordered his servant, 'Go out quickly into the streets and alleys of the town and bring in the poor, the crippled, the blind and the lame.' "'Sir,' the servant said, 'what you ordered has been done, but there is still room.' "Then the master told his servant, 'Go out to the roads and country lanes and compel them to come in, so that my house will be full. I tell you, not one of those who were invited will get a taste of my banquet.'"

IN OUR WESTERN CULTURE, educators, preachers, and others teach from a position of superiority. That is, the educator and the preacher know the answer to the question and they deliver it to you in a lecture or a sermon. Interestingly, the issue of student engagement is becoming more prevalent in higher education institutions, indicating that the more a student is engaged in the activity of learning beyond the classroom, the more the student will learn.[1]

---

1. Duzevic, "A Conceptual Framework," 69.

The Seat of Humility

A Different Way to Learn

In Judaism in the first century, teaching occurred through the asking of questions, discussion, and debate to assist disciples to work through the answer on their own.[2] The idea was, in part, that if a disciple came to a conclusion on his own, without the direction of the rabbi, the disciple was more likely to embrace the answer in the face of alternate answers. Interestingly, "[o]ne rabbi lamented the death of his stiffest opponent, because he had no one to spar with, no one who would force him to refine his thinking."[3] In our social media society, debate is a rare commodity, and friendly debate even more rare, not only among non-believers, but believers as well. It seems that believers are eager to post their dislike not just for a position, but for a person, or people with whom they disagree. Disagreement and debate are not bad, but when we as believers result to name-calling we lose something very precious along the way; we lose the ability to start a dialogue and we lose the ability to *refine our thinking*.

After healing the sick man Jesus asked the question that would shed light on the hearts of the Pharisees and scribes in attendance, "Is it lawful to heal on the Sabbath or not?"[4] Is it possible that Jesus, after asking the question if it was lawful to heal on the Sabbath, hearing no rebuttal, was disappointed?

This is a loaded teaching moment. Jesus asked the leaders of the Law seated around the table, staring at this sick man, whether it was lawful to heal on the Sabbath. In our supercharged culture of argumentation, and not the academic kind, we may see Jesus asking this question sardonically. We don't seem to be concerned about getting to the truth; after all, what really is truth? We're more concerned about being right, being the loudest, being heard. So, we place Jesus in that category, expecting him to confront the teachers of the Law with an, *answer my question or get out* kind of attitude. However, that's likely not the attitude Jesus was demonstrating,

---

2. Spangler and Tverberg, *Sitting at the Feet of Rabbi Jesus*, 33.
3. Spangler and Tverberg, *Sitting at the Feet of Rabbi Jesus*, 33.
4. Luke 14:3 (NIV).

particularly as a Jewish rabbi. It seems that Jesus was hoping for some kind of debate or at least disagreement to get to the heart of the issue. Nonetheless, the participants around the table didn't oblige Jesus.

Although the reader isn't told, the Pharisees that were present at this symposium were likely from the school of Shammai, the conservative school. As such they would have stricter views of the Sabbath than the school of Hillel. Obviously, this is speculation, though their silence and Jesus' question seem to indicate that there was some tension of disagreement in the room.

Jesus and the Pharisees

Prior to this symposium, Luke presented his readers with a series of scenes that were indicative of the Pharisees' hypocrisy. In Luke 13:1–8, Jesus told a story of a man who approached a vinedresser, concerned that the fig tree was bearing no fruit. The vinedresser asked the man to give the fig tree one more year and then if it was still bearing no fruit, cut it down. The fig tree was a symbol of Israel. Jesus said that Israel, and more specifically, the Pharisees, were not bearing fruit. In Luke 13:10–17, Jesus healed a woman on the Sabbath and after being confronted by Pharisees, he accused them of hypocrisy. In Luke 13:18–21, Jesus told stories of mustard seed and yeast in comparison to the kingdom of God. Those things that seem insignificant, small, or of no matter, will grow to fill the world in spite of the traditions and the hypocrisy of the Pharisees.

In Luke 13:22–30, Jesus told one more story of a narrow door through which people should go to enter the kingdom. When that door is shut, many will plead to be let in but will not be allowed to. Jesus here was again referring to the Pharisees as he spoke of the patriarchs and the tradition that the Pharisees kept. In spite of that, the Pharisees would not be allowed in but would be kept in the dark, where there is weeping and gnashing of teeth. Jesus here was referring not to hell, but to darkness as in outside of a banquet hall.[5] Banquets were well lit in the first century.[6] Outside, however, was darkness. If someone was removed and thrown out of a banquet it was said they were thrown out into utter darkness where there is weeping and gnashing of teeth.[7]

Finally, in Luke 13:31–35, Jesus was sorrowful for Jerusalem because they were not seeing who Jesus truly was and what he had come to do. This brings us to the symposium in Luke 14.

Healing on the Sabbath

This symposium presents Jesus teaching what appears to be three separate lessons. After all, what does healing on the Sabbath, a lesson on choosing the correct seat at the table, and a wedding banquet have in common? I've heard plenty of sermons in my lifetime that start off well, make sense, provide a thoughtful big picture idea, but then degrade into incomprehensible points, if there are any points at all. If we don't pay attention to the flow of this symposium as told by Luke, we may miss the connection that Jesus was making. Luke informs us that Jesus was being watched by the Pharisees in attendance of this symposium. If this symposium took place after the woes that Jesus delivered to the other group of Pharisees, if they were some of the same group of Pharisees and scribes, it certainly makes sense that the Pharisees and the scribes would want to keep their eyes on Jesus.

Up to this point Jesus had a tendency to do things differently than many of his contemporary religious leaders. He didn't wash his hands before he ate (Luke 11:38); he allowed a woman to behave inappropriately at the table (Luke 7:38); he ate with tax collectors and sinners (Luke 5:30). What is this man capable of, if he is willing to debase himself in these ways? It's no wonder that the Pharisees present at this symposium were watching Jesus.

---

5. "Manners and Customs."
6. "Manners and Customs."
7. "Manners and Customs."

Interestingly, Jesus seemed to be watching his host and other guests in return.[8] First things first, though, Jesus healed a man suffering from dropsy. But it was the Sabbath. Work should not be done on the Sabbath, and that includes healing, according to the Pharisees present.

Exodus 20:9–11(NIV) introduced the Sabbath to the Jews, saying:

> Six days you shall labor and do all your work, but the seventh day is a sabbath to the Lord your God. On it you shall not do any work, neither you, nor your son or daughter, nor your male or female servant, nor your animals, nor any foreigner residing in your towns. For in six days the Lord made the heavens and the earth, the sea, and all that is in them, but he rested on the seventh day. Therefore the Lord blessed the Sabbath day and made it holy.

The Jews were commanded by God to work for six days and on the seventh day, the Sabbath, to do no work, to consider the Sabbath day as holy. But what constituted work?

Nearly three hundred years before Jesus, the Pharisees were born out of necessity in reaction to Greek expansion.[9] The Pharisee party grew as a way to preserve Jewish law and culture in the face of pressure from the Greeks to assimilate to Greek culture.[10] Through the years, the Pharisees developed more rigid rules as a means to preserve Jewish Law, and to inoculate themselves from foreign culture.[11] As has been mentioned previously, these added rules became just as important as, or even more important than the Law itself, essentially becoming law. Furthermore, the rules that the Pharisees followed became more of an external function than an inward transformation.[12] So was it lawful to heal on the Sabbath?

---

8. Story, "One Banquet with Many Courses," 67–93.
9. Peterson, *Jesus Way*, 208.
10. Peterson, *Jesus Way*, 208.
11. Peterson, *Jesus Way*, 210.
12. Peterson, *Jesus Way*, 211.

Samuel Tobias Lachs says yes and no.[13] If life is in danger, then it is permissible to heal on the Sabbath, but if life is not in danger, it is not permissible to heal on the Sabbath.[14] However, this is likely a later development of the Sabbath rules. Nonetheless, did Jesus break the Law by healing the man with dropsy? The Pharisees present thought he did. Was this man's life in danger because of his dropsy? Probably not.

Healing for Jesus was far more than simply freeing a person from sickness. As was expounded upon in the previous chapter, in Luke 4:14–19, Jesus was in Nazareth's synagogue and was handed a scroll to read. Jesus read from Isaiah 6:1–2 (NIV): "The Spirit of the Lord is on me, because he has anointed me to proclaim good news to the poor. He has sent me to proclaim freedom for the prisoners and recovery of sight for the blind to set the oppressed free, to proclaim the year of the Lord's favor." This passage is related to another passage in Daniel 9 where after praying, Daniel is visited by the angel Gabriel. Gabriel says in Daniel 9:24 (NIV), "Seventy 'sevens' are decreed for your people and your holy city to finish transgression, to put an end to sin, to atone for wickedness, to bring in everlasting righteousness, to seal up vision and prophecy and to anoint the Most Holy Place."

The Daniel and Isaiah passages are indicative of what the Lord instituted in the Law as the Jubilee. Leviticus 25:8 (NIV) says, "Count off seven sabbath years—seven times seven years—so that the seven sabbath years amount to a period of forty-nine years." This year of Jubilee was to be a time of freedom from captivity, cancelation of debts, and a general making right of everything for everyone in Israel. Jesus, in Luke 4:14–19, announced himself as the Jubilee, the anointed one, mentioned by Gabriel in Daniel 9, who would free God's people. In healing the man with dropsy, Jesus was showing himself to be greater than the Pharisees and their rules; he was the true Sabbath, the Jubilee who had come to renew God's people. But the Pharisees did not see that.

---

13. Lachs, *A Rabbinic Commentary*, 199.
14. Lachs, *A Rabbinic Commentary*, 200.

Rather than wait for one of the Pharisees or scribes to ask the question, Jesus asked, "Is it lawful to heal on the Sabbath or not?"[15] If a donkey or ox were to fall into a well, Jesus said, certainly the Pharisees would pull them out. So, why not heal a sick man on the Sabbath? Luke informed us that the Pharisees and scribes had nothing to say, either because they wanted to hear what else Jesus would say to incriminate himself, or they didn't want to incriminate themselves by showing that they may not care for the sick man. Either way, the following lessons base themselves around Jesus healing the man on the Sabbath.

Let's be sure here that the Sabbath is not simply about not doing work. Often we, as Christians in our Western context, consider the Sabbath as not working. On your Sabbath, don't mow the yard, which I'm all too happy to comply with. On Your Sabbath, don't cook, but happily go to a restaurant where others are forced to work. For the Jew, the Sabbath is less about not working, but not creating; after all, God himself rested from creation on the seventh day[16] For example, lighting a candle creates a new element by the merging of the lit match and the candle.[17] Cooking creates a new substance from raw meat or vegetables being cooked on the stove or in the oven.[18] So, the Pharisees and scribes were less concerned about Jesus' *working*, and more concerned about Jesus' *recreating*.

Two Lessons

Just as the Pharisees and the scribes were intently watching Jesus, he was watching them as well. He must have noticed that some of the guests were seating themselves around the table. Seating around a first-century Jewish table indicated social standing.[19] Depending on where the guest was sat would indicate the guest's

---

15. Luke 14:3 (NIV).
16. Lancaster, *Restoration*, 118.
17. Lancaster, *Restoration*, 115–16.
18. Lancaster, *Restoration*, 115–16.
19. Story, "One Banquet with Many Courses," 82.

social standing. So, a guest who was sat at a low position would know he was socially less important than one sitting at a higher position.

In our culture today, at a banquet or symposium where a special speaker has been invited to speak, there are typically varying levels of people present. As an invited guest, it is often unlikely that you would walk up to the speaker's table and sit down, because you know that those seats have been reserved for other specially invited people. However, if as an invited guest you take a seat toward the back, and a host of the banquet or symposium asks you to be seated at the speaker's table, then you are honored. This is the scenario that Jesus referred to in his first lesson. Referring back to the man with dropsy who was healed, Jesus was essentially saying to the Pharisees to not think of themselves more highly than they ought. How are they any more special than the man Jesus just healed? Rather, the Pharisees, and we for that matter, should consider ourselves servants, taking places of lesser honor to honor those around us.

My father, who recently passed away, was the kind of person who would give his seat up to anyone if he knew it would make them more comfortable, help them see the TV better, or just simply feel more included in what was going on. When he died, he was 71 years old. Up to his dying day, he gave up his seat for those around him to make them feel more comfortable and welcomed.

Serving one another does not always come naturally. In a culture that is often marked by greed and instant gratification, service is definitely not the default position. However, Jesus came so that we would see that there is a new way, a better way to live, a way that is different, and in many ways, opposite of the culture. In this case Jesus demonstrated that service and humility are the better way.

The lesson that is being taught here is less about your position around the table, and rather about the position you take within the kingdom of God. Outside of the table, where do you place yourself? Who do you serve? Who do you expect should serve you?

My wife and I have been married for 27 happy years. We attribute our happiness to our desire to serve one another. Neither one of us sees ourselves as greater than the other. Rather, we make it a point in nearly all that we do to serve the other. This is one of the not-so-secret secrets of a happy marriage.

In what appears to be a response to Jesus' lesson, one of the guests around the table said, "Blessed is the one who will eat at the feast in the kingdom of God."[20] In other words, the guest was saying, "In spite of your story about service, and the healing of this unclean man on the Sabbath, I plan to be invited to the feast of God in his kingdom." I can just see a wry smile come over Jesus as he said, "About that, I have another story for you, and you're not going to like it."

Jesus didn't say that. But he should have. Jesus told the story of a man who held a great banquet. After having invited several people, he sent his servants out to collect them. However, the invited guests all had excuses as to why they couldn't come to the banquet. The man then instructed his servants to invite the "poor, the crippled, the blind and the lame."[21] After being told there is still more room, the man compelled his servants to "go to the roads and country lanes"[22] and bring people in, the kind of people like the man who was healed of dropsy, the man whom the Pharisees seemed to ignore apart from Jesus behaving badly on the Sabbath. The host of the banquet says, "I tell you, not one of those who were invited will get a taste of my banquet."[23]

Keep in mind the previous chapter where Luke recorded the lessons that Jesus had for the Pharisees, showing that they have caused Israel to be unfruitful and that they were hypocrites. Now Jesus told those at this symposium that though they were invited to the feast of the Lord, they, like the guests invited to the banquet, didn't show up. They weren't getting it. They didn't understand who it was who sat in front of them and that they were even now feasting with the Lord, the Messiah. They made excuses as to why they didn't understand, why they weren't following Jesus, and in

---

20. Luke 14:15 (NIV).
21. Luke 14:21 (NIV).
22. Luke 14:23 (NIV).
23. Luke 14:24 (NIV).

the end, they lost their place at the table to people like the man who was just healed of dropsy. What a turn of events.

Your Place at the Table

What is your place at the table? Have you chosen your own seat? Have you seated yourself in a place of honor, or a place of lesser honor, a place of service? The gospel writer, Mark, has been known for writing in what some have referred to as a "sandwich method."[24] In chapter 11, Jesus entered Jerusalem as the Messiah. Soon after, he walked past a fig tree that was not bearing fruit. He cursed the tree because of its lack of fruit. In chapter 12, Jesus told those present, including some Pharisees and scribes, the story of the landowner and the tenants. The tenants were told to produce fruit. They chose not to and in the end killed the landowner's son who came to address the problem. Soon after, a scribe approached Jesus and asked him the meaning of the law, to which Jesus replied, "'Love the Lord your God with all of your heart and with all your soul and with all your mind and with all your strength.' The second is this: 'Love your neighbor as yourself.'"[25] The scribe said Jesus spoke rightly, to which Jesus said, "you are not far from the Kingdom of God." So, what does the kingdom of God look like?

Perhaps we can consider the top of the Markan sandwich as Jesus addressing the failure of Israel and the religious leadership of Israel. The meat of the sandwich has Jesus answering the scribe about the meaning of the Torah and that the scribe himself was not far from the kingdom of God. For the bottom portion of the sandwich, Mark showed Jesus demonstrating the meaning of the Torah, taking upon himself the punishment due the Jews for their failure to be a light to the nations and a blessing to the world, as promised to Abraham. Jesus became the true Jew, the true human being, loving his Father God, his neighbor, and the whole earth; he

---

24. Edwards, "Markan Sandwiches," 195.
25. Mark 12:30–31 (NIV).

would give his own life in service of the purpose of Israel, to be a blessing to the whole earth.

Where does this symposium leave us? Jesus addressed the issue of image and pride with the Pharisees and scribes. Often in the church, we can be very concerned about our own image, taking care not to associate with those who we deem unclean so not to soil the good name of Christ in our own life.[26]

I can recall a particularly frustrating scenario in my life. Frustrating now, though I did not see it then. When I was working as a youth pastor at one of our church summer camps, a young man came, dressed all in black, obviously not wanting to participate in the events of the week. I remember often saying to myself, and, ashamedly, saying to some of my students who were with me at the summer camp that this young man shouldn't even have come. He was a distraction.

On Saturday morning, the morning when the campers packed up and went home after a great week of camp, I learned that this young man had made a decision to follow Jesus. Like the good hypocrite that I was, I went to the young man, shook his hand, and told him that I was glad he came to camp.

When I think about that event, I find myself filled with regret. How could I have served this young man during the week? How could I have stepped out of my concern for my own image and demonstrated the Jubilee love of Jesus in spite of his attitude and demeanor? As believers, we need to serve others in need and introduce them to the Lord of the Sabbath through our own love and service.

Questions for Reflection:

1. Typically, Christians consider Sunday to be our Sabbath. When presented with an opportunity to serve on your Sabbath, do you provide help and serve, or do you choose to stick

---

26. Kinnaman and Lyons, *UnChristian*, 123.

to your Sabbath and honor God while potentially dishonoring your neighbor?

2. As a metaphorical guest in your community, do you see yourself as an honored guest or as a servant? Why?

3. What are some ways that you can serve others around you, regardless of their position socially?

Six

The Last Supper

A Symposium?

LUKE 22:7-38 (NIV)

Then came the day of Unleavened Bread on which the Passover lamb had to be sacrificed. Jesus sent Peter and John, saying, "Go and make preparations for us to eat the Passover." "Where do you want us to prepare for it?" they asked. He replied, "As you enter the city, a man carrying a jar of water will meet you. Follow him to the house that he enters, and say to the owner of the house, 'The Teacher asks: Where is the guest room, where I may eat the Passover with my disciples?' He will show you a large room upstairs, all furnished. Make preparations there." They left and found things just as Jesus had told them. So they prepared the Passover.

When the hour came, Jesus and his apostles reclined at the table. And he said to them, "I have eagerly desired to eat this Passover with you before I suffer. For I tell you, I will not eat it again until it finds fulfillment in the kingdom of God." After taking the cup, he gave thanks and said, "Take this and divide it among you. For I tell you I will not drink again from the fruit of the vine until the kingdom of God comes." And he took bread, gave thanks and broke it, and gave it to them, saying, "This is my body given for you; do this in remembrance of me."

The Last Supper

In the same way, after the supper he took the cup, saying, "This cup is the new covenant in my blood, which is poured out for you. But the hand of him who is going to betray me is with mine on the table. The Son of Man will go as it has been decreed. But woe to that man who betrays him!" They began to question among themselves which of them it might be who would do this.

A dispute also arose among them as to which of them was considered to be greatest. Jesus said to them, "The kings of the Gentiles lord it over them; and those who exercise authority over them call themselves Benefactors. But you are not to be like that. Instead, the greatest among you should be like the youngest, and the one who rules like the one who serves. For who is greater, the one who is at the table or the one who serves? Is it not the one who is at the table? But I am among you as one who serves. You are those who have stood by me in my trials. And I confer on you a kingdom, just as my Father conferred one on me, so that you may eat and drink at my table in my kingdom and sit on thrones, judging the twelve tribes of Israel.

"Simon, Simon, Satan has asked to sift all of you as wheat. But I have prayed for you, Simon, that your faith may not fail. And when you have turned back, strengthen your brothers." But he replied, "Lord, I am ready to go with you to prison and to death." Jesus answered, "I tell you, Peter, before the rooster crows today, you will deny three times that you know me."

Then Jesus asked them, "When I sent you without purse, bag or sandals, did you lack anything?" "Nothing," they answered. He said to them, "But now if you have a purse, take it, and also a bag; and if you don't have a sword, sell your cloak and buy one. It is written: 'And he was numbered with the transgressors'; and I tell you that this must be fulfilled in me. Yes, what is written about me is reaching its fulfillment." The disciples said, "See, Lord, here are two swords." "That's enough!" he replied.

THE JEWS OBSERVE MANY feasts and festivals as spiritual and even physical representations of God's work in their lives. Leviticus 23 provides a list of the feasts and festivals the Jews were commanded to observe throughout the year, in part relating to agriculture. In our part of the world, observing special times of the year or special events in the church are easily compartmentalized in part due to influences of Greek culture. For instance, prior to the Christmas season, the observance of Advent is common among several denominations. Although many churches and Christians may observe Advent, does the meaning of Advent make its way from the church bulletin, from the candle lighting, from the singing of hymns, and the prayers, to our hearts and minds? As the Jews observed these feasts and festivals, it wasn't as easily compartmentalized; that's not how they viewed reality.[1] It was intimately integrated into their life. So, the observance of a feast or festival was truly a recognition of God's presence in their midst, his blessing, and his provision for his people.[2]

A Passover Supper?

This banquet is different from the previous banquets. Although the Passover could be considered a symposium as it is a banquet that was and still is used to teach a lesson, it is a symposium in a category all its own, a symposium where the participants dramatically relived the events of the Exodus from Egypt. However, this banquet seems to symbolize something more than the Passover, more than the Jews' escape from Egypt.

Is this meal a traditional Passover meal? Traditionally we seem to refer to this meal as a Passover meal. Luke said this is the day of Unleavened Bread when the Passover lamb was sacrificed.[3] Matthew had the disciples asking Jesus where he wanted to make preparations for the Passover.[4] Mark, like Luke, indicated that this was the day the Passover lamb was sacrificed.[5] John said the

---

1. Tverberg, *Reading the Bible with Rabbi Jesus*, 84.
2. Tverberg, *Reading the Bible with Rabbi Jesus*, 111.
3. Luke 22:7.
4. Matt 26:17
5. Mark 14:12.

meal that Jesus ate with his disciples was just before the Passover Festival.[6]

It appears that there is a discrepancy between Matthew, Mark, and Luke, and John. Some suggest that this is due to the calendar that the writers used.[7] Matthew, Mark, and Luke may have used the biblical solar calendar while John may have used the Babylonian lunar calendar of the temple.[8] Nonetheless, this means the supper that Jesus and his disciples celebrated that evening was likely a Passover supper.

Christians today celebrate communion that is based primarily on this meal with references made by Paul in 1 Corinthians 11:23–26 (NIV):

> For I received from the Lord what I also passed on to you: The Lord Jesus, on the night he was betrayed, took bread, and when he had given thanks, he broke it and said, "This is my body, which is for you; do this in remembrance of me." In the same way, after supper he took the cup, saying, "This cup is the new covenant in my blood; do this, whenever you drink it, in remembrance of me." For whenever you eat this bread and drink this cup, you proclaim the Lord's death until he comes.

The Passover supper was, and still is, a multi-faceted, highly involved supper. The Passover Seder, or order, is a specific order of reviewing the events that took place during the first Passover, the Jews' exodus from Egypt. During the Passover Seder, it was and is customary to teach those present the significance of the events of the Exodus. Later a book of readings, questions, stories, and blessings would be produced and read. This book is called the *Haggadah*. Jacob Sloan says of the order of the Passover, "In the course of the centuries, the ritual of the Seder has undergone only one decisive change: the Questions and the Haggadah recital were advanced to a position before the meal."[9] Possibly this was done so

---

6. John 13:1.
7. Throntveit, "Lord's Supper as New Testament," 279.
8. Throntveit, "Lord's Supper as New Testament," 279.
9. "Passover: 'Pesach.'"

that people could go through the *Haggadah* before they became too sleepy.

Today, the focal point of the Seder is an ornately decorated plate with the following items:

1. Green parsley dipped in saltwater or vinegar to remind the Jews of the tears shed as slaves.
2. Unleavened bread that signifies the Israelites' quick departure from Egypt. There are three layers of unleavened bread or matzah. They are stored in a three-layered bag or drawer of sorts. The second layer of bread is broken, called the *afikomen*, which is hidden away for children to find later. Some believe the *afikomen* was a symbol of the messiah and that after the meal it was this broken off piece of the matzah that Jesus gave to his disciples as his body.
3. Bitter root, normally horseradish, reminding the Jews of the bitterness of slavery.
4. An apple, honey, and nut mixture to remind the Jews of the mortar used to make the bricks.
5. A roasted egg as a reminder of renewed life.
6. A lamb shank bone, though now often beef or roast fowl, to commemorate the sacrifical lamb.[10]

The Four Cups

During the Passover there were four cups that were used to remember the Exodus.[11] The four cups comes from Exodus 6:6–7 (NIV):

> Therefore, say to the Israelites: 'I am the Lord, and *I will bring you out* from under the yoke of the Egyptians. *I will free you from being slaves to them*, and *I will redeem you* with an outstretched arm and with mighty acts of

---

10. "Passover: 'Pesach.'"
11. Routledge, "Passover and Last Supper," 210.

judgment. *I will take you as my own people*, and I will be your God. Then you will know that I am the Lord your God, who brought you out from under the yoke of the Egyptians. [Emphasis mine]

The four cups were:

1. I will bring you out;
2. I will free you from being slaves to them;
3. I will redeem you;
4. I will take you as my own.[12]

The first cup, "I will bring you out,"[13] is the cup of sanctification. The first cup symbolized the bringing out from Egypt of the Israelites, the sanctifying of the people of God.

Preparing for the Meal

Before the second cup was poured, those around the table would have washed their hands in preparation for the meal and dipped the bitter herbs into salt water. However, rather than simply ceremonially wash in preparation for the meal, John 13 (NIV) records that Jesus rose from the table and washed his disciples' feet. To do so, Jesus wrapped his clothes around him, much as the slave of the home would do, and washed their feet. Jesus, taking on the likeness of the household slave, washed his disciples' feet and told them that this was meant to be an example of the kind of life they should live, a life of service to others. Jesus was saying that true freedom is demonstrated as we freely give our lives in service to others.

Saint Patrick, the patron saint of Ireland, would agree. As a teenager, Patrick was captured by the Irish and forced to tend sheep. Patrick escaped after having a dream and returned home.

---

12. Routledge, "Passover and Last Supper," 210.
13. Exod 6:6 (NIV).

When Patrick was in his mid-forties, he returned to Ireland to serve them and lead the Irish to faith in Jesus.[14]

Love Your Enemy

Soon after washing, Jesus and the disciples would have dipped their bitter herbs in salt water, likely representing the bitter tears the Israelites shed because of their slavery.[15] It was around this time that Jesus dipped his herbs in the bowl with Judas Iscariot, the traitor. If Jesus is considered the host of this dinner, Jesus would have dipped his herbs into a bowl to his right or left. Those positions around the table were positions of honor. If Judas sat at Jesus' right or left, Judas sat at a place of honor. Consider that for a moment. Jesus knew who would betray him. He was aware, likely, the result of Judas's betrayal, Jesus' arrest and crucifixion. Yet he sat Judas in a place of honor. Jesus as the suffering servant served not only his friends, but his enemies as well.

You may recall the second law that Jesus delivered on the Sermon on the Mount in Matthew 5–7 (NIV). Jesus delivered his law by saying in Matthew 5:43–48 (NIV):

> You have heard that it was said, 'Love your neighbor and hate your enemy.' But I tell you, love your enemies and pray for those who persecute you, that you may be children of your Father in heaven. He causes his sun to rise on the evil and the good, and sends rain on the righteous and the unrighteous. If you love those who love you, what reward will you get? Are not even the tax collectors doing that? And if you greet only your own people, what are you doing more than others? Do not even pagans do that? Be perfect, therefore, as your heavenly Father is perfect.

Jesus, the great teacher, demonstrated love not just for his friends, but also for the enemy at the table who was preparing to turn him in to the authorities for thirty pieces of silver. Take some time to

---

14. Hunter, *Celtic Way of Evangelism*, 1–2.
15. Routledge, "Passover and Last Supper," 211.

reflect on that. We all have people we like, others we like less, and, if we're honest, people we may even associate as our enemies. How should we treat those that we consider our enemies? Jesus placed his enemy in a place of honor, and even washed his feet. How can, or should, you honor your enemy?

Jesus, the Lamb of God

The unleavened bread was next, though after the destruction of the temple, the unleavened bread replaced the paschal lamb as the central element of the Passover meal.[16] During Jesus' day, the paschal lamb was still the center component of the meal with unleavened bread served with the lamb and the bitter herbs.[17]

At this point of the meal, the second cup was poured, the cup of "I will free you from being slaves to them."[18] The story of the salvation of the Jews from Egypt would be retold while breaking the unleavened bread. It was at this point in the supper that Jesus broke the bread, gave it to his disciples, identifying with the unleavened bread and the Passover sacrifice. I wonder if Jesus retold the story of the Jews rescue from Egypt. I would like to think that Jesus retold the rescue from Egypt story and inserted himself into the story to help his disciples understand what was taking place. I recognize this is speculation. Nonetheless, Jesus, the lamb of God, the obedient sacrifice of the Father, would understand the incredible meaning of the Jews' rescue from Egypt, and what he was about to do.

The purpose of retelling the story of the Jews' freedom from the Egyptians was so that the participants around the table could identify with their ancestors as if they were there with them. N.T. Wright used David's defeat of Goliath as an example here. He said, "[t]he roots of this idea are in the Jewish beliefs that the king represents his people, as David represented Israel against the Philistines

---

16. Routledge, "Passover and Last Supper," 217.
17. Routledge, "Passover and Last Supper," 213.
18. Exod 6:6 (NIV).

when he fought Goliath. What is true of the king is true of them."[19] In other words, what was true of the Israelites' escape from Egypt was true of the Jews observing the Passover, including Jesus and his disciples. The difference here, though, is that Jesus expected his disciples, then and now, to identify with him, his death and resurrection. What was true of Jesus is true of his followers. With Jesus' obedience of the Father, taking upon himself first the curse of the Jews and their disobedience, and ultimately of all humanity, both Jews and gentiles share in the promises of Jesus. So what Jesus accomplished on the cross and with his resurrection, we, his followers, both Jew and gentile, have accomplished. That is truly good news!

After the meal, as Luke says, Jesus took the cup and said, "This cup is the new covenant in my blood, which is poured out for you."[20] There is a final cup, but this cup is probably not that one. After the meal the Jews would take the third cup, the cup that signified redemption. This cup, Jesus said, signified his blood. In the Passover, the cup signified the redemption of the Jews. This third cup, "I will redeem you"[21] became to the Jews around the Passover table with Jesus, for Paul in his theology, and for us today, a new exodus. An exodus from the slavery of sin and disobedience and a redemption provided by the blood of Jesus, the true paschal Lamb.

The Kingdom

The fourth and final cup was the cup that indicated that God has made for himself a people that are his own.[22] To the Jews this meant the Jews; to Jesus, this meant the whole human race—as God covenanted with Abraham in Genesis 12:3—who believe in Jesus as their Savior. For the Jew, this cup was fulfilled at Mount Sinai with the giving of the Law, the covenant made between

---

19. Wright, *Galatians*, ch. 3.
20. Luke 22:20 (NIV).
21. Exod 6:6 (NIV).
22. Exod 6:7.

The Last Supper

God and his people. To Jesus, though, this final cup represented something that was yet to take place. This final cup is the cup Jesus will not drink until we are all together finally in the kingdom of God. Until that time, though, Jesus had a cup only he could drink, the cup of suffering, his death on the cross (Matt 26:38–39; Mark 14:35–36; Luke 22:42).

Jesus retold the Passover so that the story of the Jews' escape from Egypt incorporated all of humanity, both Jew and gentile. However, the story is not about a geographical move from one part of the world to another. Rather, the story is about the leading of God's people, all of humanity who believe in Jesus, from the slavery of sin and death into the promised Kingdom of God, a fact that the disciples eating with Jesus were still unsure about because they began to squabble about who would be the greatest in Jesus' kingdom.

The kingdom the disciples were expecting was a kingdom that Jesus, the Messiah, one like King David, would set up in place of Rome. In Acts 1, after Jesus' resurrection and 40 days of accomplishing miracles, his disciples asked, "'Lord, are you at this time going to restore the kingdom to Israel?'"[23] Their sights were still focused on Jesus their Messiah reestablishing the kingdom of Israel in place of Rome. Jesus responded not with a firm rebuke, but a reminder, a contrast, of how his kingdom compares to those of the world.

Kingdoms of this world are ruled and governed by sinful, selfish humanity that are more concerned about power and control. Rather, Jesus' kingdom is filled with people who are like children eager to serve rather than to exercise power over others.

Recently, my wife and I received an encouraging text about our son. A young mother with her children and other children she was in charge of was trying to get into the front door of the public school. My son, an eleven-year-old boy at the time, eagerly opened the door for her and her entourage. When we expressed our delight in his service, he seemed confused; it's just something anyone would have done, right? In our culture, too many people are in a

23. Acts 1:6 (NIV).

hurry to get where they are going and do what they need to do. If someone is struggling around them, well, that's their problem. Rather, as Jesus said, we should be like an eleven-year-old boy who knew no other response than to serve.

What should the kingdom of God look like? Jesus demonstrated for his disciples, and for us for that matter, that the kingdom of God looks like service. We seem to get that wrong in the church. We assume the kingdom of God is about evangelism, about getting people saved, about ensuring they don't have tattoos or listen to music that some consider to be questionable. Would Jesus have been concerned about any of those things? Maybe. However, Jesus demonstrated that the kingdom of God is about serving from a heart of love and gratitude, about doing something out of love for God and a love for your neighbor.

In our Western world, it seems the impetus is on belief, on what you think. Do you know Jesus? Do you know what he says? Do you believe the particular sets of doctrines of this church? Here, Jesus showed his disciples what is important. He didn't minimize belief; after all, it was their belief that kept his disciples, and the Jews in general, coming back to Jerusalem year after year to participate in the Passover. It is because they believed it was important. Jesus said if you believe it is important, you will do something about it. If you believe the kingdom of God is upon us, how you demonstrate your belief is by serving one another.

Daily, the Jews pray a prayer that Moses taught them at Mount Sinai. They pray the Shema. The Shema starts with the words, "Hear, O Israel: The Lord our God, the Lord is one" (Deut 6:4, NIV). To hear for the Jews is far more than to listen to words; to hear means to do.[24] The Shema is prayed not to simply hear the words of the Lord, but to do the words of the Lord. Jesus' disciples understood this. Though, Jesus needed to demonstrate for them what it meant to do the kingdom of God and to do service.

James, one of the leaders of the Jewish church in Jerusalem after Jesus' ascension, wrote these words to Jewish believers about the importance of doing the word of God in James 1:22–25 (NIV):

24. Spangler and Tverberg, *Sitting at the Feet of Rabbi Jesus*, 87.

The Last Supper

> Do not merely listen to the word, and so deceive yourselves. Do what it says. Anyone who listens to the word but does not do what it says is like someone who looks at his face in a mirror and, after looking at himself, goes away and immediately forgets what he looks like. But whoever looks intently into the perfect law that gives freedom, and continues in it—not forgetting what they have heard, but doing it—they will be blessed in what they do.

The kingdom of God is advanced not simply on listening, or even simply believing, but from acting on our belief.

After the meal, Jesus turned to Simon Peter and in a moment of concern, warned Peter of portions of the trial that were to come. Jesus said, "Simon, Simon, Satan has asked to sift all of you as wheat. But I have prayed for you, Simon, that your faith may not fail. And when you have turned back, strengthen your brothers." Jesus seemed to be aware that Peter would deny him, though Jesus said, when you turn back and when you are restored as my disciple, strengthen the others who will need your encouragement and strength during the difficult times to come.

Peter responded to Jesus that he would gladly follow Jesus to his death if need be. To which Jesus said, "I tell you, Peter, before the rooster crows today, you will deny three times that you know me."[25] Robby Gallaty, in his book, *The Forgotten Jesus: How Western Christians Should Follow an Eastern Rabbi*, says that the rooster Jesus referred to is likely not the flightless foul we are accustomed to on farms, but rather refers to the temple crier who would shout out the timing of the morning service.[26] Whether the rooster was an actual bird or a temple crier, the reality remains that Peter did in fact deny Jesus. The feeling of betrayal must have been heavy in Peter's heart upon hearing the rooster. Peter seems to be an emotional sort, often responding to Jesus' statements or others with an emotional outburst. As an emotional, introspective person myself, I can imagine the feelings of guilt and shame must have

---

25. Luke 22:34 (NIV).
26. Gallaty, *Forgotten Jesus*, 193.

been nearly overwhelming, particularly knowing what was likely to happen next—the crucifixion of your rabbi.

Next, Jesus made a statement that has had commentators perplexed for years. He said to his disciples, "But now if you have a purse, take it, and also a bag; and if you don't have a sword, sell your cloak and buy one." Wait! Wasn't Jesus a pacifist? Jesus' ministry didn't seem to be one of violence. From what we have read about Jesus up to now, he hasn't been interested in overthrowing the Roman government with a violent revolution. David Lertis Matson suggests in his article, *Double-Edged: The Meaning of the Two Swords in Luke 22:35–38*, that the reference to the swords was more likely a call to be prepared for possible violence between their trek from where they were observing the Passover to the Mount of Olives, where Jesus would finally be arrested.[27] Jesus' divine destiny included Judas turning him over to the authorities, not being hijacked and killed in the interim.

If this is the case, this may be a cause to question some of our theology of determination. Is God in control? If so, couldn't he stop a group of marauders from bringing an untimely death to Jesus? Yes. However, what is happening here? God, and Jesus, seem to be acting within the boundary of human freedom and will. There is a destiny toward which Jesus is heading and that does not include being killed on the way to the cross. What does this mean for you and me? God doesn't force his way into the lives and situations of humanity but works within them. But then again, at times he does get intimately involved in the lives of humanity. What about Jonah? If it weren't for that pesky storm and fish, Jonah might have found himself safely hidden away from God's intervention. But God did get involved in a dramatic way.

So, does God directly act in nature and among humanity, or act within the boundary of human freedom and will? Yes. We don't like answers like this, but if we're honest we can see God's hand moving in our life in ways that seem inconspicuous at times, and at other times, clearly in control.

---

27. Matson, "Double-Edged," 475.

The Last Supper

Throughout the Passover dinner that Jesus celebrated with his disciples, he demonstrated that God's love and God's plans are grander and more intricate than we can imagine. What should we do? Remember our Lord Jesus, roll up our sleeves, and serve.

Questions for Reflection:

1. The Passover is the Jews' reminder that God rescued them from Egypt to take them to the promised land. Paul tells us that Christian communion is an abbreviated form of the Passover. What does it mean to you that Jesus has rescued you from sin and is leading you to the promised land of his kingdom?

2. Despite Judas being a traitor, Jesus still honored him during the Passover dinner. How can you honor those around you that you may have a difficult time getting along with?

3. Jesus put on himself the garment of a household slave and served his disciples. What can you do to serve your family? Your church? Your community?

Seven
A Meal with Two Disciples

LUKE 24:13-35 (NIV)

Now that same day two of them were going to a village called Emmaus, about seven miles from Jerusalem. They were talking with each other about everything that had happened. As they talked and discussed these things with each other, Jesus himself came up and walked along with them; but they were kept from recognizing him. He asked them, "What are you discussing together as you walk along?" They stood still, their faces downcast. One of them, named Cleopas, asked him, "Are you the only one visiting Jerusalem who does not know the things that have happened there in these days?" "What things?" he asked.

"About Jesus of Nazareth," they replied. "He was a prophet, powerful in word and deed before God and all the people. The chief priests and our rulers handed him over to be sentenced to death, and they crucified him; but we had hoped that he was the one who was going to redeem Israel. And what is more, it is the third day since all this took place. In addition, some of our women amazed us. They went to the tomb early this morning but didn't find his body. They came and told us that they had seen a vision of angels, who said he was alive. Then some of our companions went to the tomb and found it just as the women had said, but they did not see Jesus."

A Meal with Two Disciples

He said to them, "How foolish you are, and how slow to believe all that the prophets have spoken! Did not the Messiah have to suffer these things and then enter his glory?" And beginning with Moses and all the Prophets, he explained to them what was said in all the Scriptures concerning himself.

As they approached the village to which they were going, Jesus continued on as if he were going farther. But they urged him strongly, "Stay with us, for it is nearly evening; the day is almost over." So he went in to stay with them. When he was at the table with them, he took bread, gave thanks, broke it and began to give it to them. Then their eyes were opened and they recognized him, and he disappeared from their sight. They asked each other, "Were not our hearts burning within us while he talked with us on the road and opened the Scriptures to us?"

They got up and returned at once to Jerusalem. There they found the Eleven and those with them, assembled together and saying, "It is true! The Lord has risen and has appeared to Simon." Then the two told what had happened on the way, and how Jesus was recognized by them when he broke the bread.

MANY, IF NOT ALL, of us have lost someone special to us. Whether it be a relative or a friend, hearing of the loss can be a confusing time, making us wonder, what is happening? What could have been done to keep this from happening? In 1995, one week after I graduated from college, I learned that my mother had unexpectedly passed away. My father called me, asked me if I was sitting down, and delivered the devastating news. I was 25 years old and did not expect that my mother would die so soon. I recall heading home with my wife where I sat in a chair most of the evening in a bit of a stupor. Fast forward to 2018. My stepmother called me early in the morning on July 15, informing me that my dad had a massive heart attack and it wasn't looking good. My wife, our kids, and I made the trek to Illinois and watched as my dad, unconscious and unresponsive, slowly passed away.

Jesus' Table Talk

Two Disciples Walk With Jesus

These two disciples, likely not two of the original twelve, were on their way to Emmaus. They had just lost their rabbi, the one they believed would change everything. These two disciples wouldn't have been traveling the day before as it was the Sabbath. The Sabbath for the Jews is a day of joy, a day of celebration.[1] Though it makes you wonder what must have been going through the disciples' minds, including these two, after their rabbi, their Messiah, was killed.

At the beginning of this book I indicated that banquets and symposia would be the primary table references addressed. This reference is neither a banquet nor a symposium. However, we will find here a significant lesson that can be learned before, during, and after the table.

While the disciples were on their way to Emmaus, Jesus approached them and began to walk with them. It seems that the disciples didn't recognize Jesus, or that they were kept from recognizing him. I have had a perpetual problem with remembering people, both faces and names. Just this fall, a friend of mine whom I had attended undergraduate studies with, approached me and asked if I remembered her. I had to admit that I did not. Even more, I didn't even recognize her. Likely this wasn't a divinely inspired lack of recognition. Nonetheless, it was embarrassing.

In this case, these two disciples who likely had spent some time with Jesus, enough to at least recognize Jesus and be considered his disciples, had a conversation with him about the horrible travesty of the loss of their teacher. Jesus began to teach these disciples what was taught in the Law and the prophets. At this point it would be advantageous to review the timing of three important feasts that would have taken place during this time. Whether Jesus used these feasts as the backdrop for his teaching with these disciples, we don't know. Nonetheless, these feasts provide important elements in the death and resurrection of Jesus.

---

1. Fung, "Sabbath," 316.

A MEAL WITH TWO DISCIPLES

The Feast of Unleavened Bread

The first feast would be the Passover that was reviewed in the last chapter. Jesus celebrated the Passover with his twelve disciples just three days prior to this. Jesus provided a different interpretation to some elements of the Passover story—that his blood was represented by the cup of redemption and that his body was represented by the unleavened bread of the Passover meal. The day after the Passover meal was the Feast of Unleavened Bread. In Exodus 12:17–20 (NIV), we read:

> Celebrate the Festival of Unleavened Bread, because it was on this very day that I brought your divisions out of Egypt. Celebrate this day as a lasting ordinance for the generations to come. In the first month you are to eat bread made without yeast, from the evening of the fourteenth day until the evening of the twenty-first day. For seven days no yeast is to be found in your houses. And anyone, whether foreigner or native-born, who eats anything with yeast in it must be cut off from the community of Israel. Eat nothing made with yeast. Wherever you live, you must eat unleavened bread.

The Feast of Unleavened Bread was observed in commemoration of the Israelites' flight from Egypt. Because their exodus was quick, they didn't have the time to allow yeast to activate and dough to rise. 1 Corinthians 5:8 (NIV) gives some hints into the meaning of this feast when Paul wrote, "Therefore let us keep the Festival, not with the old bread leavened with malice and wickedness, but with the unleavened bread of sincerity and truth." In this passage, for Paul, the yeast was a symbol of wickedness, while unleavened bread was a symbol of sincere worship of God. Furthermore, Jesus' body is that bread that unites all of his people, Jew and gentile, under one name, the perfect, sinless name of Jesus the Messiah.

Jesus' Table Talk

The Feast of Firstfruits

On this day, the day after the Feast of Unleavened Bread, these two disciples were walking from Jerusalem to Emmaus, a seven-mile journey. On this day the Jews would have celebrated the third feast of this season, the Feast of Firstfruits. The ordinance of the Feast of Firstfruits is recorded in Leviticus 23:9–14 (NIV):

> The Lord said to Moses, "Speak to the Israelites and say to them: 'When you enter the land I am going to give you and you reap its harvest, bring to the priest a sheaf of the first grain you harvest. He is to wave the sheaf before the Lord so it will be accepted on your behalf; the priest is to wave it on the day after the Sabbath. On the day you wave the sheaf, you must sacrifice as a burnt offering to the Lord a lamb a year old without defect, together with its grain offering of two-tenths of an ephah of the finest flour mixed with olive oil—a food offering presented to the Lord, a pleasing aroma—and its drink offering of a quarter of a hin of wine. You must not eat any bread, or roasted or new grain, until the very day you bring this offering to your God. This is to be a lasting ordinance for the generations to come, wherever you live.

According to verse 10, this Feast of Firstfruits is about the harvest, a first offering to God as Lord of the harvest. The Jews were to bring this offering in the promised land, not in the wilderness because it was in the promised land that they would begin the agricultural responsibilities of sowing and reaping. There were disagreements between the Pharisees and the Sadducees on the day the firstfruits were to be offered.[2] The Pharisees considered that the Passover was a Sabbath.[3] So, the day after Passover, the Feast of Firstfruits was to be given. The Sadducees did not hold that view.[4] Rather, after the Sabbath, after Passover, the Feast of Firstfruits was given. For us, it doesn't really matter. For them, it was a big deal. No bread or roasted grain was to be eaten until the offering was given. In the context

---

2. Parsons, "Wave Sheaf Offering."
3. Parsons, "Wave Sheaf Offering."
4. Parsons, "Wave Sheaf Offering."

of the two disciples, the Passover would have been celebrated on Friday, the Feast of Unleavened Bread would have started on the day after Passover, the Sabbath. The Feast of Firstfruits would have been celebrated on this day, the day the two disciples were making their way to Emmaus.

It is likely that these two disciples would have celebrated the Feast of Firstfruits while in Jerusalem. However, soon after the offering of the firstfruits, they began to make their way to Emmaus.

The Feast of Firstfruits was to be a feast observed by the Jews as a lasting ordinance, meaning, essentially, forever. However, according to the author of Hebrews, the Son, Jesus, is superior to the angels and to Moses, the giver and receiver of the Torah (Heb 1, 3). Jesus as the sacrificial lamb has brought into and through himself the full meaning of the festivals and feasts, accomplishing their fullness in himself (Heb 2:14–16).

As believers, often when we hear the term *harvest* in the context of Scripture, we are drawn to evangelism and mission. After all, the fields are ripe for harvest. The harvest that is spoken of here, though, is a harvest that follows the firstfruits of the harvest. The first fruit of the harvest is Jesus, the first offering to God as the first resurrected and renewed of humanity.

According to a proposed timeline for the offering, a member of the Sanhedrin, during Jesus' day, would bind a sheaf of the first grain of the harvest to prepare it as an offering to God.[5] When it was time to present to the Lord, the grain would be cut and brought to God on the day after the Sabbath and wave it before the Lord.[6] It is assumed that the night the member of the Sanhedrin bound the grain was also the night Jesus was bound in preparation for his crucifixion.[7] On the day that Jesus rose, the day after the Sabbath, he became the firstfruits offering to God.

Jeremiah 2:3 indicates that Israel was the first fruit of God. Jeremiah said, "'Israel was holy to the Lord, the firstfruits of his harvest, all who devoured her were held guilty, and disaster

---

5. Parsons, "Wave Sheaf Offering."
6. Parsons, "Wave Sheaf Offering."
7. Parsons, "Wave Sheaf Offering."

overtook them,' declares the Lord."[8] The story of Israel in this Jeremiah passage is a sad one. God redeemed his people from Egypt, presenting them to himself as firstfruits in the promised land. But they strayed from God. Another first fruit was needed, one that would be presented to God as the perfect, sinless first fruit. The interesting thing about the firstfruits offering of a harvest is that there is more harvest to come. If there is more harvest to come, it becomes clear that not only are the Jews the harvest, but all of humanity. It is from the seed of Abraham that all of the people of the earth will be blessed.[9]

So, let's look at the timing of the feasts to this point:

1. Passover—Jesus died for the sins of the world as the sinless, perfect Lamb of God on the day of the feast.

2. Feast of Unleavened Bread—The true character is shown of the sinless son of God who shed His blood as a sacrifice for the sins of the world. Only those who put their faith and trust in the finished work of the one who embodies righteous, the Lamb of God, the Messiah, will be given eternal life.

3. Feast of First-Fruits—He fulfilled this feast by being resurrected on the day of the feast of firstfruits.

So, what does it mean that Jesus was resurrected on the day of the Feast of Firstfruits? 1 Corinthians 15:20-23 (NIV) says, "But Christ has indeed been raised from the dead, the firstfruits of those who have fallen asleep. For since death came through a man, the resurrection of the dead comes also through a man. For as in Adam all die, so in Christ all will be made alive. But each in turn: Christ, the firstfruits; then, when he comes, those who belong to him."

What is Paul saying here? Paul is arguing that there will be a resurrection from the dead for all believers and that Jesus was the firstfruits of that resurrection. However, there were other resurrections in Jesus' day, resurrections that Jesus accomplished

---

8. Jer 2:3 (NIV).
9. Gen 12:3.

A Meal with Two Disciples

for others. For instance, Lazarus (John 11) and Jairus's daughter (Mark 5). What makes Jesus the first fruit? Paul addressed this in 1 Corinthians 15:50–56 (NIV):

> I declare to you, brothers and sisters, that flesh and blood cannot inherit the kingdom of God, nor does the perishable inherit the imperishable. Listen, I tell you a mystery: We will not all sleep, but we will all be changed— in a flash, in the twinkling of an eye, at the last trumpet. For the trumpet will sound, the dead will be raised imperishable, and we will be changed. For the perishable must clothe itself with the imperishable, and the mortal with immortality. When the perishable has been clothed with the imperishable, and the mortal with immortality, then the saying that is written will come true: 'Death has been swallowed up in victory.' 'Where, O death, is your victory? Where, O death, is your sting?' The sting of death is sin, and the power of sin is the law.

Jesus was the first fruit of the resurrection, meaning there are more resurrections to come. The more to come are you and I. Jesus who died perishable rose imperishable. We too will die perishable and will rise imperishable. As Paul says in 2 Thessalonians 2:13–14 (NIV):

> But we ought always to thank God for you, brothers and sisters loved by the Lord, because God chose you as first fruits to be saved through the sanctifying work of the Spirit and through belief in the truth. He called you to this through our gospel, that you might share in the glory of our Lord Jesus Christ.

The Thessalonian church was predominantly a gentile church. They were firstfruits of the salvation harvest who were also promised to be resurrected as renewed people just as Christ was resurrected and renewed as the first fruit of all creation.

Was the lesson of the firstfruits part of the lesson Jesus taught the disciples on their way to Emmaus? We don't know. But we do know that Jesus taught these disciples from the Torah and the prophets of the necessity of the Messiah to die and to be raised again. This brings us to the table fellowship in the village.

At the table, the disciples still did not recognize who Jesus was, that he was their teacher. However, as Jesus broke bread, their eyes were opened. Leviticus 23:12, 14 says that the people of Israel were not to eat bread until the sacrifice of the lamb without defect and the offering of the firstfruits was given. As Jesus, the spotless lamb and first fruit of all creation, broke bread with these disciples, the eyes of the disciples were opened to who Jesus was. He was the pure spotless lamb, the firstfruits of all creation, the Messiah who came to fulfill the promise given to Abraham, to be a blessing to all of Israel and to all of humanity.

As we break bread with one another, we must be reminded that Jesus is the firstfruits of our salvation, which includes our resurrection and renewal. As the disciples headed back to Jerusalem and testified to the other disciples all they saw and heard from Jesus, we should do the same. We must testify of the hope of resurrection and renewal of humanity and of all creation.

Questions for Reflection:

1. What does it mean to you that Jesus was the first fruit of the resurrection?
2. As believers, we can walk through difficult times in our lives. How can we make sense of those times knowing that Jesus is walking with us?
3. How can you use the table as an opportunity to help other people's eyes to open to the reality of who Jesus is?

Eight
From Jesus' Table to Ours

IF THE TABLE IS a place where character and behavior can be checked and encouraged, certainly Jesus' table is no exception. The lessons that Jesus presented at table challenged and encouraged the people of Jesus' day and should challenge and encourage us today as well. Over the next few pages we'll review the table encounters in our own context and ask ourselves, *how should I respond?*

The Least, the Lost, and the Outcast

In Jesus' first table encounter, he attended a banquet held by the local tax collector. Tax collectors were the outcasts by choice. They colluded with the Roman government in spite of their Jewish heritage, and so were seen as no longer a part of the Jewish community. It was at this banquet that Jesus, a respected rabbi, attended, accepting Levi as one of his disciples, a person no one else would dream of accepting.

As Christians, we can find ourselves in similar circumstances as that of the Jews, including the Pharisees—legitimately concerned that people we may come into contact with will have a bad influence on us or on others, not to mention the reputation we may earn for spending time with people like that. Because of this, we shouldn't look so poorly on the Pharisees who likely were concerned that Jesus was building a bridge with someone dangerous and downright sinful.

Is there a different perspective we should have? Is it really an either/or proposition? In one of Jesus' final commands to his disciples, he said, "All authority in heaven and on earth has been given to me. Go therefore and make disciples of all nations, baptizing them in the name of the Father and of the Son and of the Holy Spirit, and teaching them to obey everything that I have commanded you. And remember, I am with you always, to the end of the age" (Matt 28:18–20, NIV). Jesus gave this command to his group of disciples. Within this group was a tax collector, brothers with aggression issues, and a fisherman who had the habit of saying and doing the wrong thing at the wrong time. Not exactly the group of people you would want on your leadership team. As disciples of Jesus, the men would have understood Jesus' command. "Just as I have called people like you to follow me, so you call people like you to follow you as you follow me." Go into all the world and seek out people like the disciples. Consider this: Jesus also called Judas to be his disciple. Judas's failure to follow Jesus isn't the issue; rather, the reality is that Jesus called Judas, knowing that he would ultimately fail.

As disciples and followers of Jesus, you and I don't have that luxury to know if someone will follow through on their commitment to Jesus. Our responsibility is simply to follow Jesus and invite others to follow him as well, despite our limited perspective on the chances of that person fulfilling their commitment.

As Jesus instructed in his sermon in Matthew 5:13–16, followers of Jesus are to be salt and light. Salt has an interesting flavor and preserving quality. On the one hand, salt added to food draws out more of the flavor of the food. I love to cook hamburgers. When I was younger, I enjoyed a more well-done burger. As time has come and gone, give me a medium rare with a little salt and pepper and I am a happy man. Likewise, salt is a preservative. It draws out extra water on food, so bacteria won't form.[1] As preservers and flavor-ers, we followers of Jesus have a responsibility

---

1. Helmenstine, "Why Does Salt Work as a Preservative?"

to provide a preserving and flavoring quality for one another, for those we are ministering to, and for our culture.

As preservers we are a sort of conscience, modeling faith and love to keep ourselves and those around us in check. Francis Schaeffer said:

> What we are called to do, upon the basis of the finished work of Christ in the power of the Spirit through faith, is to exhibit a substantial healing, individual and then corporate, so that people may observe it.[2]

We are called to preserve and to bring healing to those around us in our culture. This can only be done through contact—through going into our world and preaching and living the gospel in every part of our lives.

In Acts 26, Luke records that Paul stood before Festus and King Agrippa defending himself against the accusations of some of the Jewish leadership who were calling for Paul to be executed. Paul provided Agrippa and those watching with the account of his encounter with Jesus and subsequent response to follow Jesus. After Paul provided his version of his call to follow Christ, Agrippa asked in Acts 26:28 (NIV), "Are you so quickly persuading me to become a Christian?" To which Paul responded in verse 29: "Whether quickly or not, I pray to God that not only you but also all who are listening to me today might become such as I am—except for these chains." Paul was salt and light for the culture to which he was ministering.

With that in mind, light has qualities to which Jesus may have been alluding in his Sermon on the Mount in Matthew 5. Psalm 112:1–4 (NIV) says this about light:

> Praise the Lord! Happy are those who fear the Lord, who greatly delight in his commandments. Their descendants will be mighty in the land; the generation of the upright will be blessed. Wealth and riches are in their houses, and their righteousness endures forever. They rise in

---

2. Schaeffer, *Trilogy*, 165.

the darkness as a light for the upright; they are gracious, merciful, and righteous.

Also, in Psalm 119:105 (NIV), the Psalmist says, "Your word is a lamp to my feet and a light to my path." The light of the righteous lights up the darkness, and God's word leads the righteous as a lamp in a dark place. Light expels the darkness, making a path easier to see. Light exposes dark places helping us to see where we need to go. As lights in a dark place, and salt in a dying world, we are called by Jesus to be light and salt in a dark, flavorless, decaying world.

Unexpected Interruptions

In Jesus' second table encounter, a symposium at the Pharisee Simon's house, Jesus was greeted by an unexpected interruption: a woman barged into the meal scene, kissing Jesus' feet, crying tears on his feet, and wiping his feet with her loose hair. Not knowing for sure what sort of woman this was, we do know she was inappropriate, interrupting a meal normally designated for men. With confidence, though, we can say this interruption was unexpected.

Interruptions are rarely welcomed. On an average day, whether we plan out our day or work on tasks as they come, interruptions are difficult to manage. I admit I have a tendency to have a particular path in mind, and when something comes along to move me from my path, or even suggest a move, I mentally wrestle with myself and the interruption. My wife has admitted that she has planted seeds of change in my mind weeks in advance of actually making that change, all so I'll manage the change better for myself and for the family.

I understand that the interruption that occurred at table in Simon's house with Jesus was a bit different than what I described above, though it was an interruption. Possibly it's not just about the interruption, but who was interrupting. This woman was, well, a woman. Possibly she was a prostitute or a reformed prostitute. Possibly she was in mourning after the loss of a loved one.

Regardless, she had something she needed to do for Jesus, and she needed to do it now! In so doing, she demonstrated hospitality when Simon did not.

Being a person of hospitality and good manners is not innate. Children are not born with the ability to show hospitality. Jesus commended the party-crashing woman for greeting him while Simon the Pharisee, who should know better, did not greet Jesus properly, thus not showing hospitality. Despite who this woman was, she was more of a host than Simon was.

Showing hospitality is an important characteristic to demonstrate as a follower of Christ. The first and greatest example of hospitality was that of Abraham and his wife in Genesis 18:6–8, who cared for the three visitors who came to address the sin of Sodom and Gomorrah. Abraham and his wife prepared three *seahs*—thirty-six pounds—of flour for bread, and had one of his own finest calves prepared for the meal.

Interestingly, we discover that Sodom and Gomorrah were condemned in part because of their lack of hospitality. In Ezekiel 16:49–50 (NIV), the Lord said, "Now this was the sin of your sister Sodom: She and her daughters were arrogant, overfed and unconcerned; they did not help the poor and needy. They were haughty and did detestable things before me. Therefore I did away with them as you have seen." Amongst other things, Sodom was destroyed because of their lack of care of those in need; they did not show hospitality.

In Matthew 25, Jesus told the parable of the sheep and the goats. After dividing out the sheep and goats, he said to the righteous, "For I was hungry and you gave me something to eat, I was thirsty and you gave me something to drink, I was a stranger and you invited me in, I needed clothes and you clothed me, I was sick and you looked after me, I was in prison and you came to visit me."[3] To which the righteous asked when it was that they cared for and fed Jesus. Jesus said, "Truly I tell you, whatever you did for one of the least of these brothers and sisters of mine, you did for me." As we show hospitality to one of the least of these, we show

3. Matt 25:35–36 (NIV).

hospitality to Jesus—a lesson Simon the Pharisee had not learned, but a lesson that the woman, one of the least of these, understood.

Another important lesson that is taught at this table is that of forgiveness and thankfulness. The parable Jesus told Simon reminded him that the debtor who had more to pay than the other was more thankful for the forgiveness of the debt. The unexpected party crasher had a greater debt that was forgiven by Jesus, so she responded with greater thankfulness. In our own lives, we have great debts that we cannot pay, debts of sin and disbelief. Jesus forgave our debts. We are drawn to our Savior in gratitude for the great debt he has lifted from us. As we have been forgiven, so we forgive.

As such, another debt that we may have is that of love toward one another. In response, Paul said in Romans that the only debt that should remain is the debt of love.[4]

Burdens or Blessings

The lesson learned at Jesus' third table encounter in Luke, when Jesus confronted the Pharisees and scribes present of the burdens they heaped on others, is that of being a burden or being a blessing. Jesus seemed clear that the Pharisees and scribes expected so much from the Jews, but in many cases they themselves weren't willing to live according to those expectations that the Jews couldn't live up to. This was not an issue of the leaders of the Law expecting that the Jews live according to the Law, as sometimes we as Christians assume. Living according to the Law was expected. Jesus wasn't angry at the Pharisees and scribes for expecting the people live according to the Torah. Rather, Jesus was angry that the teachers of the Law expected that the Jews live according to other traditions and teachings outside of the Torah.

Jesus was interested in bringing the Jews back to the basics, back to the foundation of their relationship with God: the Torah, the prophets, and the writings, that is, the Old Testament. A

---

4. Rom 13:8.

misunderstanding we as Christians have is that Jesus came to do away with the Old and replace it with the New. Reading through some of Jesus' statements in his Sermon on the Mount, we may gather that Jesus was interested in reinterpreting some of the commands in the Torah. Rather, it seems that Jesus was interested in helping his listeners understand the meaning of the Torah.

Jesus said in his famous sermon in Matthew 5:17–18 (NIV):

> Do not think that I have come to abolish the Law or the Prophets; I have not come to abolish them but to fulfill them. For truly I tell you, until heaven and earth disappear, not the smallest letter, not the least stroke of a pen, will by any means disappear from the Law until everything is accomplished.

As believers today, we like to point to this passage and say, "See, Jesus came to do away with the Law; if it's been fulfilled it's been completed and no longer needed, right?" Not really. The hint comes for us in verse 18; after Jesus said he came to fulfill, he also said that not even the smallest accent marks on the words written in the Law will disappear until all things are accomplished. Jesus came not to do away with the Law, but to live it out correctly, to interpret the Law rightly.[5]

As Christians, we can often find ourselves requiring certain kinds of behavior, certain kinds of dress, hairstyle, and so on, based on our own interpretation of what we believe the Bible is saying. Kinnaman and Lyons in their book, *UnChristian*, relay several concerns people have had regarding their experience with Christians. One story he tells of Victoria,

> Everyone in my church gave me advice about how to raise my son, but a lot of the time they seemed to be reminding me that I have no husband—and besides, most of them were not following their own advice. It made it hard to care what they said. They were not practicing what they preached[6].

5. Hays, "Applying the Old Testament Law Today," 29.
6. Kinnaman and Lyons, *UnChristian*, 43.

A young lady in a church near us recently went through a difficult divorce. Though her church didn't ask her to leave, they also didn't seem to be very supportive. The stigma of divorce was far too great for them than the need to show love and acceptance. As Western Christians, we seem to live in a tension of what is absolutely right and what is absolutely wrong. To assume that there may be a gray area within that tension is tantamount to heresy. That's the way God sees it, right? Truth is black and white with no room for gray. Well, not exactly.

The Bible seems clear enough that lying is wrong. One of the Ten Commandments reminded the Jews not to "bear false witness against your neighbor" (Exod 20:16, NIV). Proverbs 14:25 (NIV) says, "A truthful witness saves lives, but one who utters lies is a betrayer." However, in Joshua 2, Rahab the prostitute of Jericho hid the Israelite spies and lied to the soldiers when they came to look for them. Isn't lying a sin? Ye, Rahab is mentioned in Hebrews 11 among the other great witnesses of faith. Was it right? Was it wrong? Is there a gray area?

Middle Eastern cultures, including those during Jesus' day, were less concerned about absolutes and more concerned about relationships.[7] Right and wrong was less of an issue, and relationship was vastly important. In Galatians, Paul vehemently teaches the Galatians that circumcision is not needed to be part of the covenant Christ has reestablished (Gal 5). However, in Acts 16, Paul circumcised Timothy so he wouldn't lose face with the Jews in the area. In Paul's case, in both Galatians and Acts, the issue was not absolutes but relationship. Jesus has opened the door of fellowship between the Father and the rest of the gentile world. As gentiles, we have access to God through Jesus, not circumcision.

As followers of Christ today, we often place rules above relationship. Certain kinds of behavior, certain kinds of attire, and certain kinds of voting patterns should be immediately accompanied with a person when they choose to follow Jesus. This can cause frustration, disillusionment, and ultimately deciding not to follow Jesus. Rather, if relationships come first, what should our response

---

7. O'Brien and Richards, *Misreading Scripture with Western Eyes*, 166.

be? Love the sinner. We often follow that up with: hate the sin. Sometimes, though, that can get confusing for us and for those we are trying to love. Instead, simply love the sinner. Does that mean we tolerate the sin and overlook it? No. But neither do we condemn; after all, that's not our job. Love the sinner and journey with them closer to a relationship with Jesus. In so doing, you just may find yourself getting closer to Jesus, too.

A Servant in the Kingdom

What lesson can be learned from Jesus' encounter with the Pharisees and scribes around the table on the Sabbath as Jesus healed a man, encouraged a rearrangement of the seating pattern, and told a story of a big banquet? Frankly, a significant lesson can be learned. First, it is important to keep in mind that it is the Sabbath. Second, it is important to keep in mind that the seating arrangement around a table in first-century Palestinian culture indicated the person's social status.

Jesus healed a man who was likely watching the dinner proceedings taking place. Whether he was brought there by others or came on his own, we are not told. Could he have been placed there by the Pharisees to test Jesus? Again, we are not told and it is unnecessary to speculate. Jesus healed this man, reminding those in attendance that they would rescue a donkey or a child from a well. Why is this man's life any different? The greater good, in this case, is to heal the sick man, which Jesus did.

Jesus then taught a lesson of personal placement in social structures. Noticing that some of the guests chose their own seat, he challenged them to choose a seat of lower status. Finally, Jesus told the story of a man who invited several people to a banquet, though the people he invited chose not to come. The man then chose to invite people to the banquet much like the sick man Jesus just healed, indicating that those who were originally invited would not be able to attend.

The meaning seems clear. How do you see yourself in contrast to other people around you? Do you see yourself as more important? Better than everyone else? Whether the person in question is sick, a different gender, a different sexual orientation, a different religion, or a different political persuasion, how do you size yourself up in contrast to that person?

From the beginning, the Sabbath was created as a time to acknowledge God and his creation, as well as to care for the rest that others should have in God. In Exodus 20:8-11 (NIV), God said:

> Remember the sabbath day, and keep it holy. Six days you shall labor and do all your work. But the seventh day is a sabbath to the Lord your God; you shall not do any work—you, your son or your daughter, your male or female slave, your livestock, or the alien resident in your towns. For in six days the Lord made heaven and earth, the sea, and all that is in them, but rested the seventh day; therefore the Lord blessed the sabbath day and consecrated it.

The Sabbath was created not only for the Jews, but for those outside of the Jewish nation and for all of creation. The Sabbath is not simply a time to not do any work. It is also a time to honor others, regardless of their station in life, to honor and care for them as God has cared for us. This idea of the Sabbath should be something that we carry with us every day and everywhere.

Paul reminds us of the importance of honoring others in Philippians 2:1-4 (NIV) when he said:

> If then there is any encouragement in Christ, any consolation from love, any sharing in the Spirit, any compassion and sympathy, make my joy complete: be of the same mind, having the same love, being in full accord and of one mind. Do nothing from selfish ambition or conceit, but in humility regard others as better than yourselves.

The Sabbath is expressed in our love for one another, our care for one another, honoring others above ourselves. As God commanded the Jews to honor not only their own, but foreigners living among them as well, we also are to honor others outside our immediate familial, religious, and social contexts. But what does that look like?

As gentile believers in Jesus we are recipients of the covenant God made with Abraham, to be blessed by Abraham's offspring (Gen 12:1–3). As recipients of this blessing, we too are to be blessings to those outside our religious and social barriers, just as Abraham's offspring were to be a blessing to the world. How can you be a blessing to those around you, those that you may not necessarily see yourself socializing with, or even accepting? It's good that you pray for them. But is that enough? Paul didn't say, "In your own prayer life regard others as better than yourselves." Rather, he seemed to be challenging his readers to act out this kind of selfless love for others in real, tangible, concrete ways. How will you live out this kind of love? It seems an important question to ask. After all, if you are invited to the banquet, but don't show up saying, "I'll pray about it," will the Father invite someone else who will live out his love?

The Final Lesson

The final lesson, the lesson at the table of the Passover, is not the final lesson that we will be looking at. However, it is the final major lesson Jesus gave to his followers collectively in Luke. This lesson hinges on the exodus, the yearly symposium of sorts, that the Jews observe to remember how God rescued them from the Egyptians and preserved them through the desert to bring them to the promised land. Rather than rewrite the story of the exodus, though, Jesus refocuses the meaning of the story of God and the Jews to Jesus and his disciples, and ultimately to the world.

Reading the story of the Passover meal in Luke and in the other Gospels, you might conclude that Jesus was rewriting the Passover dinner. The Gospel writers don't indicate that the entire Passover meal was eaten, nor, for that matter, do they indicate that the entire meal was not eaten. Rather, specific references to cups and bread were made. As such, we may feel prompted to conclude that Jesus didn't observe the Passover, but instituted a new meal, what we often call the Lord's Supper, which communion is patterned after in the Christian church.

Jesus' Table Talk

An issue we as Christians should be aware of is that communion is not a Passover Seder, nor should it be. Rather, according to Throntveit, communion is a representation of the new covenant made by Jesus to his followers.[8] This may imply that the dinner that Jesus observed with his disciples was not a Passover Seder. However, Marcus suggests that in first-century Israel the Passover Seder was not necessarily standardized, and was not so until after AD 70.[9] Likely, what was recorded in the Gospels as the Lord's Supper was a Passover dinner with specific references highlighted by Jesus for the sake of assertion as part of a new covenant.

These perspectives Jesus provided of the elements of the Passover are less a new covenant than a reestablishment of the original covenant communicated in a new way to the disciples present. God rescued his people from Egypt for a particular purpose. Not simply to lead them to the promised land, but to fulfill the promise, the covenant, he made with Abraham in Genesis 12:1–3 (NIV), that in Abraham "all the peoples on earth will be blessed through you." When God rescued his people from Egypt, he was keeping his covenant. When God gave the Jews the Torah, he was keeping his covenant. Though his people turned from God over and over, God kept his covenant and, through his Son, the Messiah, he finally accomplished what the Jews were not able to do, that is to keep the covenant between God and his chosen one to be a blessing to the whole world.[10]

Matthew 28 and Mark 16 record Jesus commissioning his disciples to go into the world to fulfill the promise made by God to Abraham and preach the gospel. What, though, does preaching look like? In our part of the world and in our Greek-influenced culture, preaching looks like a person standing in front of a group of people declaring God's word to them. This isn't wrong, and possibly partly what Jesus had in mind. Though we must remember that Jesus was not Greek, nor did he have twenty-first-century America in mind when he gave his commission to his disciples.

8. Throntveit, "Lord's Supper as New Testament," 285.
9. Marcus, "Passover and Last Supper Revisited," 323.
10. Wright, *Surprised by Scripture*, 211.

From Jesus' Table to Ours

Jesus was Jewish and his disciples were Jewish. To understand what Jesus meant when he challenged his disciples to preach, we must understand Jesus' culture.

Possibly the best image of discipleship in first-century Judaism and Christianity is found in 1 Thessalonians 1:2–10 (NIV):

> For we know, brothers and sisters loved by God, that he has chosen you, because our gospel came to you not simply with words but also with power, with the Holy Spirit and deep conviction. You know how we lived among you for your sake. You became imitators of us and of the Lord, for you welcomed the message in the midst of sever suffering with the joy given by the Holy Spirit. And so you became a model to all the believers in Macedonia and Achaia—your faith in God has become known everywhere. Therefore we do not need to say anything about it, for they themselves report what kind of reception you gave us. They tell how you turned to God from idols to serve the living and true God, and to wait for his Son from heaven, whom he raised from the dead—Jesus, who rescues us from the coming wrath.

Paul provided an outline for his readers of the discipling process. As missionaries to a foreign culture, Paul and his companions not only preached but lived the gospel of Jesus in front of the Thessalonians, demonstrating through conviction and integrity the life of Christ. Paul said, "This is what a believer in Jesus looks and acts like, now you go and do likewise," and they did. The Thessalonians followed Paul and his companion's example and imitated the life that Paul modeled. Furthermore, the Thessalonians modeled their faith for others to follow as well. Paul was so overjoyed at the faith of the Thessalonians because he heard it from other people to whom the Thessalonians ministered and discipled.

This outline of discipleship provides the perspective of the first-century rabbi and disciple.[11] The rabbi models, the disciple imitates. The disciple becomes a rabbi who models for his disciples who imitate, and the pattern goes on and on. As believers today,

---

11. Spangler and Tverberg, *Sitting at the Feet of Rabbi Jesus*, 80.

we have the blessed opportunity to live a life of commitment to Christ, to be a model to others in our context. In so doing, we lead others to imitate us as we imitate Christ. As they become followers of Jesus, they in turn become models for others to follow. Though this is a simplistic version of the expectation of discipleship, I believe it is a biblical version, one we would do well do emulate.

Another table lesson the Passover can teach us is that God is interested not only in rescuing his people out of something, but rescuing them for something. God's promise to Abraham to be a blessing to the world was ultimately fulfilled in and through Jesus. However, Jesus included his followers in the fulfillment of the promise by sending them (and us) out to the world.

N.T. Wright, in *Surprised by Hope*, outlines for the believer the importance of understanding that the church is not rescued out of this world, but rescued to be a blessing for the world.[12] Just as the Jews were called from the time of Abraham to bless the world, so we, who have been grafted into the faith, the calling, and the promises of God, are likewise to be a blessing to the world. This blessing is not only for spiritual renewal, but for physical, social, and psychological renewal as well.[13] By all means this is not a propagation of kingdom theology; rather, this is a recognition of the promises made by God to his people to be a blessing to the world. We share in the blessing as the blessed and the blessers. Through Jesus we are blessed by his obedience and sacrifice, and we bless the world, preaching the now and coming renewal of all of creation (Rev 21:1–7).

The now renewal of creation is not a complete renewal. This will not come until Christ finally renews the heaven and the earth (Rev 22:1–7). The now renewal encompasses how we live out the Christian faith amongst our families, friends, neighbors, and world. Paul presents a picture of what this renewed life should look like from us to the world in Romans 12:9–21 (NIV) when he says,

---

12. Wright, *Surprised by Hope*, 197.
13. Wright, *Surprised by Hope*, 211.

Love must be sincere. Hate what is evil; cling to what is good. Be devoted to one another in love. Honor one another above yourselves. Never be lacking in zeal, but keep your spiritual fervor, serving the Lord. Be joyful in hope, patient in affliction, faithful in prayer. Share with the Lord's people who are in need. Practice hospitality. Bless those who persecute you; bless and do not curse. Rejoice with those who rejoice; mourn with those who mourn. Live in harmony with one another. Do not be proud, but be willing to associate with people of low position. Do not be conceited. Do not repay anyone evil for evil. Be careful to do what is right in the eyes of everyone. If it is possible, as far as it depends on you, live at peace with everyone. Do not take revenge, my dear friends, but leave room for God's wrath, for it is written: 'It is mine to avenge; I will repay,' says the Lord. On the contrary: 'If your enemy is hungry, feed him; if he is thirsty, give him something to drink. In doing this, you will heap burning coals on his head.' Do not be overcome by evil, but overcome evil with good.

The renewed life does not look like the world, like America, like Egypt, but like Jesus. The renewed life seeks to restore relationships. The renewed life seeks the place of a servant to honor others. The renewed life commits to finding a better way to confront conflict rather than to cause harm to the other. The renewed life seeks what is best for God's creation, for his creation is good.

Neither Hopeless nor Alone

The final lesson that Jesus means to teach us at the table is the lesson learned by two of his disciples on the road to Emmaus. These two disciples were not from the twelve, though they followed Jesus and considered him to be their teacher. Luke informs his readers that these two disciples were on the road to Emmaus on the same day, the Sunday that Jesus resurrected. Emmaus was about seven miles from Jerusalem so a walking journey would have taken a while. We aren't told the time of day, but likely it is earlier in the day and they wouldn't want to be caught walking in the dark for fear of bandits. As the disciples were talking with one another, Jesus appeared and began speaking with them. Scripture tells us that the two disciples were kept from recognizing Jesus. Were they kept from recognizing him because of some veil God had laid over their hearts and minds? Were they kept from recognizing him because of their own doubt and lack of understanding? Possibly this was to give Jesus the opportunity to walk with them through the Old Testament and reveal what Scripture said about him and his destiny.

Throughout our lives we may find ourselves wandering, doubting, and unsure of what path we are on. In my own life, I grew up as a Lutheran in Illinois. I attended a Lutheran school and a Lutheran church until I was 12 years old. My mother and father divorced when I was young, and after their divorce my mother began attending university. She applied to the University of Washington and moved herself, my sister, and me to Seattle. We left the church and for all intents and purposes I found myself wandering. Between my mother's agnostic bent and my father's strong Christian commitment, I found myself confused and questioning. I tended to lean more towards disbelief because that's where I lived most of the time. However, the summer after my graduation from high school, Jesus walked with me on my road, explained who he was, and led me to a firm understanding of himself in Scripture.

Likely, many people find themselves on similar roads—unsure of the events of the past, possibly walking with people who know Jesus, but never really understanding the implications of who Christ is and what difference he makes in life, faith, and the world. Possibly you or someone you know has found themselves on a journey questioning the events in their lives and trying to make sense of it all.

Take some time to sit with them, visit with them about your own journey, or if it is you wandering, listen to other people's journey. Gather together at the table, figuratively or literally, and listen to the story of Christ and how he has revealed himself in the lives of those who are searching and in the lives of those who have found him.

Nine
Conclusion

FOR THE FIRST-CENTURY JEW, the table was an important fixture among their family and their community. It was at table around which community was practiced, encouraged, and sustained. It was at table around which members of the community were entertained. It was also at table around which lessons were taught and learned.

It seems that the benefit of the table has all but been lost in our culture. If the table is a metaphor for the lessons taught and learned in life, it seems that not only are the lessons not being taught at the table, they're not being taught anywhere in the home.[1] Parents, if they are present at all in the home, seem less likely to impress on their children the word of God at any time throughout an average day.[2] When left to their own devices, young people can do some very unwise and unsafe things.[3] This is one reason why the presence of adults in the lives of young people is so important.[4] Adults serve as checks and balances for bad behavior.[5] However, parents today don't serve that purpose. Rather they tend to be emcees in

1. Haynes, *Shift*, ch. 1.
2. Haynes, *Shift*, ch. 1.
3. DeVries, *Family-Based Youth Ministry*, 35.
4. DeVries, *Family-Based Youth Ministry*, 40.
5. DeVries, *Family-Based Youth Ministry*, 40.

the lives of their children: introducing the next new, cool thing to come along and keep their children entertained.

As a community of faith, it is important for us to take the table back. If the table is a metaphor for Christian life and discipleship, as families it is our responsibility to be Christian examples not only in the home but in the community. What are some ways we as families can begin to take the table back in our homes?

Church

One way to take the table back is by actively attending church together as a family. I understand that church is not the hope of the world, Christ is. However, it is in the local church that Christ is preached and experienced with other believers together as a community of faith. If we are truly interested in affecting change in our home and at the table, we must learn to come together as believers, sharpen one another (Prov 27:17), and encourage one another into good deeds for the sake of the gospel (Heb 10:24). We accomplish this by intentionally meeting together (Heb 10:25).

Service

Another way to take the table back is to serve together as a family. Whether serving at a local para-church ministry, in the church, or simply in the community, service can be a strong bonding opportunity between family members and with Christ. In *Passing on the Faith*, Merton Strommen and Richard Hardel discovered that young people who are active in service activities in their community are more likely to continue in their faith.[6] Young people participating in ministry with adults is an effective means of discipleship, growing in faith, and learning from one another in a strong community of faith.

---

6. Strommen and Hardel, *Passing on the Faith*, 252.

CONCLUSION

The Table

Yet another way of taking the table back is to do just that: reclaim family time as an important part of your experience together. Spending time with one another where advice can be shared, care can be given, and love can be displayed, is an invaluable part of living life together and drawing closer to one another and to Christ. Mark DeVries states in *Family-Based Youth Ministry*,

> There is a table spirituality that is central to our faith. From the Jewish family rituals of the Passover and the Sabbath to the Lord's Supper and even to the banqueting table of our Lord in heaven, the undercurrent of a family meal is consistent. It is startling to realize the lack of programmatic focus in Jesus' ministry. He had no organizational chart, no planning team, no curriculum, and no ten-year long-range mission statement. Jesus' first priority in calling his disciples was 'that they might be with him' (Mk 3:14).

In Deuteronomy 6:4–9 (NIV), Moses instructed the Israelites what they must do to in their allegiance to God and their care of one another. Moses said,

> Hear, O Israel: The Lord our God, the Lord is one. Love the Lord your God with all your heart and with all your soul and with all your strength. These commandments that I give you today are to be on your hearts. Impress them on your children. Talk about them when you sit at home and when you walk along the road, when you lie down and when you get up. Tie them as symbols on your hands and bind them on your foreheads. Write them on the doorframes of your houses and gates.

Essentially, God expected his people to keep his word in front of them at all times, and to teach and encourage everyone in their households to do the same. The word Moses used to get the Israelites' attention was the word *Shema* meaning "hear" in Hebrew.[7] The word "hear" is more than just hearing the words coming from

---

7. Tverberg, *Walking in the Dust of Rabbi Jesus*, 33.

a person's mouth, it is also doing what is said.[8] To hear God's word is to be committed to doing what God's word says. With that in mind, as communities of faith, we have the responsibility to teach one another God's word and to challenge one another to do what God said we should be doing. Part of this responsibility includes coming together at the table.

Set Your Table

As believers, we have the distinct opportunity to be representatives not only of healthy families, but of Jesus Christ to our families and communities. Throughout Jesus' table lessons, he taught his disciples, his observers, and us as well, that life lived with God is more than intellectual belief, but interpersonal action as well. Jesus' table lessons teach us that life is lived not only with believers, but also within our communities, demonstrating the love and acceptance of our rabbi, our master, our Lord and Savior, Jesus.

The bottom line is that the table in the family home, as well as the table within the Christian community, must be rediscovered. So, invite friends and family over to participate in conversations and learning experiences about Christ.

---

8. Tverberg, *Walking in the Dust of Rabbi Jesus*.

Bibliography

Ahamed, Liaquat. "How Bernard Madoff Did It." *New York Times* (May 13, 2011). https://www.nytimes.com/2011/05/15/books/review/book-review-the-wizard-of-lies-bernie-madoff-and-the-death-of-trust-by-diana-b-henriques.html.

Andert, Darlene. "Alternating Leadership as a Proactive Organizational Intervention: Addressing the Needs of the Baby Boomers, Generation Xers, and Millennials." *Journal of Leadership, Accountability, and Ethics* 8 (2011) 67–83.

Baker, Elizabeth. "My Evangelical Church is Gaslighting Me, But I Refuse to Fall For it Anymore." *Huffington Post* (November 28, 2018). https://www.huffingtonpost.com/entry/evangelicalchristians-trump_us_5bfc326de4b03b230fa57ae9.

"Being a First-Century Disciple." https://bible.org/article/being-first-century-disciple.

Bergsma, John S. "The Year of Jubilee and the Ancient Israelite Economy." *Southwestern Journal of Theology* 59 (2017) 155–64.

Bruno, Christopher R. ""Jesus is Our Jubilee" . . . But How? The OT Background and Lukan Fulfillment of the Ethics of Jubilee." *JETS* 53 (2010) 81–101.

Cavanaugh, Maureen B. "Private Tax Collectors: A Roman, Christian, and Jewish Perspective." http://www.taxhistory.org/thp/readings.nsf/cf7c9c870b600b9585256df80075b9dd/a5321448c7e17ff185256f0a0059a4ba?OpenDocument.

Cosgrove, Charles H. "A Woman's Unbound Hair in the Greco-Roman World, With Special Reference to the Story of the 'Sinful Woman' in Luke 7:36–50." *Journal of Biblical Literature* 124 (2005) 675–92.

DeVries, Mark. *Family-Based Youth Ministry*. Downers Grove, IL: InterVarsity, 2004.

Dorey, E., et al. "Children and Television Watching: A Qualitative Study of New Zealand Parents' Perceptions and Views." *Child: Care, Health and Development* (2009) 414–20.

Duzevic, Ines. "A Conceptual Framework for Analysing the Impact of Influences on Student Engagement and Learning." *Tertiary Education and Management* 21 (2015) 66–79.

Bibliography

Edwards, James R. "Markan Sandwiches: The Significance of Interpolations in Markan Narratives." *Novum Testamentum* 31 (1989) 193–216.

Eisenbaum, Pamela. *Paul Was Not a Christian: The Original Message of a Misunderstood Apostle.* New York: HarperCollins, 2009.

Falk, Harvey. *Jesus the Pharisee: A New Look at the Jewishness of Jesus.* Eugene, OR: Wipf and Stock, 1985.

Fardouly, J., et al. "Social Comparisons on Social Media: The Impact of Facebook on Young Womens Body Image, Concerns, and Mood." *Body Image* 13 (2015) 38–45.

Frymer-Kensky. Tikva, *Reading the Women of the Bible.* New York: Schocken, 2002.

Fung, Christopher. "Sabbath: A Biblical Understanding of Creation Care." *Evangelical Review of Theology* 36 (2012) 316–31.

Gallaty, Robby. *The Forgotten Jesus: How Western Christians Should Follow an Eastern Rabbi.* Grand Rapids, MI: Zondervan, 2017.

Hahne, Harry. *The Corruption and Redemption of Creation: Nature in Romans 8.19–22 and Jewish Apocalyptic Literature.* New York: T & T Clark, 2006.

Harbin, Michael A. "Jubilee and Social Justice." *Journal of the Evangelical Theological Society* 54 (2011) 685–99.

Haynes, Brian. *Shift: What it Takes to Finally Reach Families Today.* Carol Stream, IL: Tyndale, 2009.

Hays, J. Daniel. "Applying the Old Testament Law Today." *Bibliotheca Sacra* 158 (2001) 21–35.

Helmenstine, Anne Marie. "Why Does Salt Work as a Preservative?" https://www.thoughtco.com/why-does-salt-work-as-preservative-607428.

Hirsch, Emil G., et al. "Feet, Washing Of." http://www.jewishencyclopedia.com/articles/6051-feet-washing-of.

Hunter, George G. *The Celtic Way of Evangelism.* Nashville, TN: Abingdon, 2010.

"The Importance of Family Dinners VII." The National Center on Addiction and Substance Abuse (2012).

"Jewish Practices & Rituals: Hospitality." Jewish Virtual Library. https://www.jewishvirtuallibrary.org/hospitality-in-judaism.

Jones, Timothy Paul. *Family Ministry Field Guide: How the Church Can Equip Parents to Make Disciples.* Indianapolis: Wesleyan House, 2011.

King, Karen L. *What is Gnosticism?* Cambridge, MA: The Belknap Press of Harvard University Press, 2003.

Kinnaman, David, and Gabe Lyons. *UnChristian: What a New Generation Really Thinks About Christianity . . . and Why it Matters.* Grand Rapids, MI: Baker, 2007.

Klein, Gil P. "Torah in *Triclinia*: The Rabbinic Banquet and the Significance of Architecture." *The Jewish Quarterly Review* 102 (2012) 325–70.

Lachs, Samuel Tobias. *A Rabbinic Commentary on the New Testament.* Hoboken, NJ: Ktav, 1987.

Bibliography

Lancaster, D. Thomas. *Restoration: Returning the Torah of Moses to the Disciples of Jesus*. Read by D. Thomas Lancaster. Newark: Audible, 2016.

Lazonby, David. "Applying the Jubilee to Contemporary Socio-Economic and Environmental Issues." *Journal of European Baptist Studies* 15 (2016) 30–50.

Levine, Amy-Jill. *Short Stories by Jesus: The Enigmatic Parables of a Controversial Rabbi*. Read by Donna Postel. Newark: Audible, 2017.

Lipnick, Jonathan. "Did Jesus Neglect to Wash His Hands Before Supper?" Israel Institute of Biblical Studies. https://blog.israelbiblicalstudies.com/holy-land-studies/did-jesus-neglect-to-wash-his-hands-before-supper/.

"Manners and Customs: Banquets and Feasts—Banquets and Expensive Feasts in the Ancient World." https://www.bible-history.com/links.php?cat=39&sub=413&cat_name=Manners+%26+Customs&subcat_name=Banquets+and+Feasts.

Marcus, Joel. "Passover and Last Supper Revisited." *New Testament Studies* 59 (2013) 303–24.

Marshall, Mary J. "Jesus: Glutton and Drunkard?" *JSHJ* 3 (2005) 47–60.

Matson, David Lertis. "Double-Edged: The Meaning of the Two Swords in Luke 22:35–38." *Journal of Biblical Literature* 2 (2018) 463–80.

McLaren, Brian D. *More Ready than You Realize: Evangelism as Dance in the Postmodern Matrix*. Grand Rapids, MI: Zondervan, 2002.

"Meal Hand-Washing." https://www.chabad.org/library/article_cdo/aid/607403/jewish/Meal-Hand-Washing.htm.

Moxnes, Halvor. "Honor and Shame." *Biblical Theology Bulletin: Journal of Bible and Culture* 24 (1993) 167–76.

Neyrey, Jerome H. "Reader's Guide to Meals, Food and Table Fellowship in the New Testament." University of Notre Dame. https://www3.nd.edu/~jneyrey1/meals.html.

O'Brien, Brandon J., and E. Randolph Richards. *Misreading Scripture with Western Eyes: Removing Cultural Blinders to Better Understand the Bible*. Read by Allan Robertson. Newark: Audible, 2014.

Ochs, Elinor, and Merav Shohet. "The Cultural Structuring of Mealtime Socialization." *New Directions for Child and Adolescent Development* 111 (2006) 35–49.

Parker-Pope, Tara. "The Family Meal is What Counts, TV On or Off." *The New York Times*. https://www.nytimes.com/2007/10/16/health/16well.html.

Parsons, John J. "The Wave Sheaf Offering." https://www.hebrew4christians.com/Holidays/Spring_Holidays/First_Fruits/first_fruits.html.

"Passover: 'Pesach.'" *Jews for Jesus*. https://jewsforjesus.org/jewishresources/community/jewish-holidays/passover-pesach/.

Peterson, Eugene. *The Jesus Way*. Grand Rapids, MI: Eerdmans, 2011.

Routledge, Robin. "Passover and Last Supper." *Tyndale Bulletin* 53 (2002) 203–21.

Schaeffer, Francis. *Trilogy*. Wheaton, IL: Crossway, 1990.

Schams, Christine. *Jewish Scribes in the Second-Temple Period*. Sheffield, England: Sheffield Academic, 1998.

Bibliography

Sjorgren, Steve, et al. *Irresistible Evangelism: Natural Ways to Open Others to Jesus*. Loveland, CO: Group, 2004.

Smith, Dennis Edwin. *From Symposium to Eucharist: The Banquet in the Early Christian World*. Minneapolis, MN: Augsburg Fortress, 2003.

Spangler, Ann, and Lois Tverberg. *Sitting at the Feet of Rabbi Jesus*. Grand Rapids, MI: Zondervan, 2009.

Steele, E. Springs. "Luke 11:37–54: A Modified Hellenistic Symposium." *Journal of Biblical Literature* 103 (1984) 379–94.

Story, Lyle. "One Banquet with Many Courses (Luke 14:1–24)." *Journal of Biblical and Pneumatological Research* 4 (2012) 67–93.

Strommen, Merton P., and Richard Hardel. *Passing on the Faith: A Radical New Model for Youth and Family Ministry*. Winona, MN: Saint Mary's, 2000.

Sweet, Leonard. *The Bad Habits of Jesus: Showing Us the Way to Live Right in a World Gone Wrong*. Naples, FL: Tyndale, 2016.

———. *From Tablet to Table: Where Community and Identity Is Found*. Colorado Springs, CO: NavPress, 2014.

Thacker, Justin. "Three Concepts of Tolerance." *European Journal of Theology* 24 (2015) 66–76.

Throntveit, Mark A. "The Lord's Supper as New Testament, Not New Passover." *Lutheran Quarterly* 11 (1997) 271–89.

Tverberg, Lois. *Walking in the Dust of Rabbi Jesus: How the Jewish Words of Jesus Can Change Your Life*. Grand Rapids, MI: Zondervan, 2012.

Ulrich, Dean R. "The Need for More Attention to Jubilee in Daniel 9:24–27." *Bulletin for Biblical Research* 26 (2016) 481–500.

Vander Laan, Ray. "Rabbi and Talmidim." https://www.thattheworldmayknow.com/rabbi-and-talmidim.

Wellhausen, Julius. *The Pharisees and Sadducees*. Macon Georgia: Mercer University Press, 2001.

Whelan, Matthew Philipp. "Jesus is the Jubilee: A Theological Reflection on the Pontifical Council for Justice and Peace's Toward a Better Distribution of Land." *Journal of Moral Theology* 6 (2017) 204–29.

Wright, Christopher J.H. "Theology of Jubilee: Biblical, Social and Ethical Perspectives." *Evangelical Review of Theology* 41 (2017) 6–30.

Wright, N.T. *Galatians: 10 Studies for Individuals or Groups*. Downers Grove, IL: InterVarsity, 2010.

———. *Surprised by Hope: Rethinking Heaven, the Resurrection, and the Mission of the Church*. New York: HarperCollins, 2008.

———. *Surprised by Scripture: Engaging Contemporary Issues*. New York: HarperCollins, 2014.

Young, Brad H. *Jesus the Jewish Theologian*. Peabody, MA: Hendrickson, 1995.

www.ingramcontent.com/pod-product-compliance
Lightning Source LLC
Chambersburg PA
CBHW071449160426
43195CB00013B/2057